CATHERINE
OF SIENA

CATHERINE OF SIENA

Passion for the Truth
Compassion for Humanity

selected spiritual writings

edited, annotated and introduced by
Mary O'Driscoll, O.P.

New City Press

Published in the United States by New City Press
202 Comforter Blvd, Hyde Park, NY 12538
©1993/2005 New City Press

Cover painting: *Catherine of Siena* by Sr. Mary Grace Thul, O.P.
Cover design by Durvanorte Correia.

Library of Congress Cataloging-in-Publication Data:

Catherine of Siena, Saint, 1347-1380.
[Selections. English. 1993]
Saint Catherine—passion for the truth, compassion for humanity :
selected spiritual writings / edited and annotated by Mary
O'Driscoll.

Includes bibliographical references.
ISBN 1-56548-235-2
1. Spiritual life—Catholic authors.   I. O'Driscoll, Mary.
II. Title.
BX2349.C2852513   1993
248.4'82—dc20   93-2543

1st printing: September 1993
7th printing, new ed.: August 2005
8th printing: January 2010
9th Printing: February 2013

Printed in the United States of America

Contents

Introduction

Catherine of Siena, whose writings we shall reflect on in this little book, lived over six hundred years ago. We may well ask what is the point of returning to the fourteenth century to get help for ourselves today, and what a young Italian laywoman who lived so long ago could possibly have to say to us. There are several answers to these questions.

It is frequently remarked that there are many similarities between our times and the times in which Catherine of Siena lived. Both periods are characterized by upheaval, change, insecurity and fear concerning the future. The fourteenth century, which saw the beginnings of the Renaissance, was a time in which much of the security of the Middle Ages was coming to an end both in state and Church. It was also a time of many wars, of natural calamities, of famine, and of terrifying sickness, including the Black Death (bubonic plague) which hit Italy the year after Catherine was born, and spread rapidly through the rest of Europe decimating the population. Part of its terror was the fact that nobody knew what its cause or remedy was. The Church of the fourteenth century was one in which many had lost faith; there was much corruption, decadence, bribery and infidelity, particularly among the clergy.[1] Before Catherine died, the schism had broken out leaving Christendom split in two.

Although we may see ourselves as more enlightened than our fourteenth century counterparts, many of their concerns and anxieties are also ours. Today we are experiencing disruption and fluctuation to a degree unknown in the past. Wars and hostilities between nations and ethnic groups are on the increase. Poverty, hunger, oppression and homelessness raise their heads in countless forms among the poor and marginalized of the world; while at the same time, greed, materialism, violence, political corruption and economic domination are evident among the powerful. Over all of us hang the threats of nuclear

---

1. In her *Dialogue* (cc. 110-34), Catherine of Siena describes with much detail the scandalous and sinful situation of the Church of her day.

destruction and ecological disaster. The AIDS epidemic is seen by many as our Black Death. The Church of our day is undergoing its own trials and difficulties with the result that for many it is no longer the safe secure haven it was before the Second Vatican Council.

Catherine of Siena had much to say that was relevant and helpful to her contemporaries. There is a good chance therefore that she can speak to us too. This chance is enhanced by the fact that in our century she has officially been given the title "Doctor of the Church," a title which recognizes the perennial value of her theological teaching.[2] We can therefore approach this laywoman from Siena with eagerness and confidence asking her our questions. We will find that she can give us satisfactory answers, not necessarily rounded and conclusive, but of such a kind that we are encouraged in a new way to continue in our pursuit of truth and love.

Catherine's Life

Who is this young woman of whom we expect so much? Catherine Benincasa was born in Siena in 1347, the twenty-third child of her parents, Jacopo and Lapa. Her father was a cloth-dyer and many of his sons joined him in this trade. Her childhood and adolescence were spent in a happy, bustling family atmosphere in which she was surrounded not only by many sisters and brothers, but also by an increasing number of nieces and nephews. From many sources we learn that she was a warm, affectionate person. As she grew older, she decided not to marry but to dedicate her life to God as a Dominican "Mantellata."[3]

Catherine's choice of the Dominican Order and, at the same time, her decision not to enter one of its enclosed monasteries are significant. She lived in the shadow of the impressive church of St. Dominic in Siena. It was the church where she prayed, celebrated the liturgy, received the sacraments, and listened to sermons. From her earliest

---

2. Catherine Benincasa was declared a doctor of the Church by Paul VI in 1970. We will explore the significance of this declaration later when we discuss her writings.

3. The Mantellate were a group of laywomen who belonged to the Dominican Order. They wore the white tunic and black mantle (hence their name) of the Dominicans and followed a Dominican Rule.

days, therefore, she knew a close familiarity with the Dominican friars
and with their special ecclesial vocation to preach the gospel. She
obviously fell in love with St. Dominic. In her *Dialogue*, she describes
him as "an apostle in the world" who sowed God's word wherever
he went, "dispelling darkness and giving light."[4] Catherine saw this
as her vocation too. It was a vocation which took her to many places
and down many different roads, often causing her much suffering,
but which she remained faithful to all her life.

After joining the Mantellate, Catherine spent three years at home
in almost unbroken solitude. It was a time of intense prayer in which
she received many graces from God. During this period, we are told,
she developed a very close relationship with Jesus Christ to whom
she used to speak "as one friend to another."[5] So great was her
intimacy with God that she was reluctant to leave her solitary life of
prayer at the end of the three years, even though she understood that
God was asking her to do so. She was afraid that if she mixed again
among people, she might lose some of her contemplative spirit. In
prayer she told God of her fears, and received the magnificent and
reassuring answer:

> I have no intention whatever of parting you from myself,
> but rather of making sure to bind you to me all the closer by
> the bond of your love for your neighbor. Remember that I
> have laid down two commandments of love: love of me and
> love of your neighbor. . . . It is the *justice* of these two com-
> mandments that I want you now to fulfill. *On two feet you
> must walk my way.*[6]

From that time on, Catherine walked firmly on the two feet of love
of God and love of neighbor, of prayer and action. Having learned the
need for two feet in her own life's journey, she is very anxious, as is
clear from her writings, to share this insight with others. In fact, one
of her greatest contributions to Christian spirituality is her insistence
on the truth that love of God and love of neighbor are inseparable in

---

4. See *Dialogue* 158. In this same chapter, she describes the Dominican Order
   as "very spacious, gladsome and fragrant, a most delightful garden."
5. This and other details concerning Catherine's life have come to us through
   her biographer, Raymond of Capua, the Dominican friar who was her
   friend, confessor and counsellor (cf. Raymond of Capua, *The Life of
   Catherine of Siena*, henceforth *Life*).
6. Raymond of Capua, *Life* II, 1, 121.

the Christian life, to such an extent that not only can one not exist without the other, but that they increase and decrease in like proportion. Many of the selections which appear in the following pages bear this out.

When Catherine first returned to the world of activity, she devoted herself to the ordinary kinds of service which women of her day did. In her family home, she helped with the many household chores that were always there to be done; and outside, in her native city, she nursed the sick, and cared for the poor. After some time, however, she realized that she was being asked to take on a wider ministry, namely, to act as peace-maker between feuding families and warring Italian states. This peace-making role took her out of Siena to other cities like Pisa and Florence and involved her in political activity. Catherine's ministry of peace-making which assumed ever greater proportions, is one of the most important aspects of her life. Through it, she was aware that she was following the example of the greatest peace-maker, Jesus Christ, who as the "bridge" between God and humanity restores the peace that has been lost through sin. In her *Dialogue* she describes Jesus as the one who reconciles humanity to God in peace, and further makes the point that those who "take his task upon themselves" are each "another Christ crucified."[7]

In 1376, at the request of the rulers in Florence, Catherine went to Avignon where the pope, Gregory XI, was residing, to make peace between the Florentines and the papacy. While she was there, she availed of the opportunity to urge the pope to return to Rome, his episcopal see. Later in that same year, Gregory XI brought the papacy back to Rome, but he died soon afterward. His successor was Urban VI who initiated many types of Church reform. However, he so displeased his cardinals that many of them turned against him. In their displeasure they went as far as to declare his election invalid, and consequently elected a new pope, Clement VII. This was the beginning of the great schism that sundered the western Church in two, and caused division in countries, cities, religious orders, dioceses and even families. Catherine suffered greatly because of the schism, and for the last eighteen months of her life her role of peace-maker

---

7. Cf. *Dialogue* 146 (henceforth D). The concept of Christ as the bridge stretching between heaven and earth is central to Catherine's christological teaching. In her writings she develops this image at length. Cf. D 21, 26-29, 59-63.

was completely taken up with trying to restore unity to the Church. From this period of her life come her most impassioned prayers and letters, as she pleaded with God, and with everyone who would listen for an end to the schism. Her greatest act at this time was to offer her life for the Church. Her prayer of self-offering is recorded in her last letter to Raymond of Capua:

> O eternal God, receive the offering of my life in this mystic body of holy Church. I have nothing to give except what you have given me, so take my heart and squeeze it out over the face of the bride.[8]

Catherine Benincasa died in Rome, to which she had come at the request of Urban VI who needed her prayerful support, in 1380. She was declared a saint in 1461 by Pius II.

Catherine the Theologian

In 1970 the pope, Paul VI, declared Catherine of Siena, *Doctor Ecclesiae, Doctor of the Church*.[9] This title has been conferred on relatively few Christian theologians in the course of Church history, and on no woman before 1970. The significance of this declaration is immense, for it places this unschooled woman among the major Church theologians, thereby recognizing her ecclesial role as a teacher whose doctrine is relevant for the whole Church and for all time.[10]

In his homily elevating her to the doctorate, Paul VI makes special mention of Catherine of Siena's "lucid, profound and inebriating absorption of divine truths," and of her "charism of exhortation" which enabled her to communicate words of wisdom and of knowledge (cf. 1 Cor 12:8). Her lucid and profound grasp of the truth was the consequence of another charism which she received from the Holy

---

8. Letter 371 (henceforth L). Tommaseo suggests that this letter was addressed to Pope Urban VI, but there is now general agreement that she sent it to her confessor and friend, Raymond of Capua (cf. Foster and Ronayne, *I, Catherine*, 271).
9. The full text appears in AAS LXII 10 (1970): 673-78. An English translation is available in *L'Osservatore Romano* (English edition), October 15, 1970, 6-7. In 1970, Teresa of Avila was likewise declared a Doctor of the Church.
10. The title *Doctor Ecclesiae* which dates back to the Middle Ages, affirms the combination of extraordinary holiness and outstanding doctrine in a particular person.

Spirit, and which is referred to by Paul VI as a "mystic charism." This charism enables those who possess it to understand divine truths not only with their faith-enlightened intellect but also affectively through their union with God. Catherine speaks of this affective knowledge as a light which brings clarity even to the light of faith. With this light, she tells us, she herself has been able to taste and see the depths of the Trinity (D 167). She highlights the experiential dimension of mystical knowledge also in her *Dialogue* when she states that those who are gifted with it "taste it and know it and experience it and feel it in their very souls" (D 61).

The theology which Catherine offers us in her writings has its source in her mystical knowledge. To make this assertion does not mean that she did not in any way have to acquire her theological knowledge. It is true that she did not receive any formal schooling, and that she learned to read only when she was already a Dominican Mantellata, and to write even later in her life. Consequently, her theological learning cannot be said to be the result of long years of study and research. At the same time, however, Catherine was a remarkably intelligent and perceptive person who had a retentive memory. It is most probable, therefore, that her "learning" came to her through oral sources, for example, through the liturgy, through the preaching of the Dominican friars in their near-by church, through the popular theological and devotional books which were read aloud in her home, and through the conversations she had with the theologians among her followers, particularly with Raymond of Capua. That she was an attentive listener is evident from her rich knowledge of scripture and from her familiarity with certain patristic and medieval themes.

Catherine's method of doing theology can be described as a process whereby she, using her gifts of nature and grace, reflected prayerfully on what she received from others, developing it and clothing it with her own language, images and penetrative insights. In her manner of being a theologian she is an excellent example of the principle that any person genuinely trying to live the Christian life, who has an active faith and a reflective attitude, can do theology.[11] In declaring

11. The International Theological Commission makes this point in its text, "Theses on the relationship between the ecclesiastical magisterium and theology," published in Latin in *Gregorianum* 57 (1976), 548-63.

the laywoman, Catherine of Siena, a Doctor of the Church, Paul VI is surely recognizing this principle.

Catherine of Siena's written works are not extensive.[12] In fact there are just three: the *Dialogue*, her *Letters* and her *Prayers*.[13] These works do not present a logically developed doctrinal system, yet they do show that Catherine's theological thought has its own inner consistency and unity, as well as its own organization and sequences.[14] The central theme in all her writings is the love of God for humankind manifested in Christ crucified. In the light of this mystery she discusses the great truths of the Christian faith: the Trinity, creation, redemption, the Church, grace, life after death. As we read her writings, we discover that, while her life may present us with extraordinary phenomena, her teaching deals with the ordinary way of holiness open to all Christians: the way of faith, hope and love. She writes to Francesco, a tailor in Florence:

> The way has been made. It is the doctrine of Christ crucified. Whoever walks along this way ... reaches the most perfect light. (L 249)

All her theology and spirituality are concerned with this way. She follows its every turn from its fearful, faltering beginning to its last stage of transforming union.

Self-Knowledge

The context in which Catherine of Siena develops her theology is her quest for self-knowledge. In the opening sentences of the *Dialogue*, she describes herself as "dwelling in the cell of self-knowledge in order to know better God's goodness toward her."[15] It is in this cell

---

12. Although we speak of Catherine's written works, it is useful to remember that while all of them were composed by her, most were not actually committed to writing by her; rather they were dictated. Several of her followers could read and write, and they acted as her secretaries.
13. More details concerning each of these works will be given later as an introduction to each of the three sections and in the bibliography.
14. This is particularly true of the *Dialogue* which Catherine planned in some detail. In a letter to Raymond of Capua (L 272), she had set down in advance the basic plan of this book.
15. D 1. Raymond of Capua states that self-knowledge is "the fundamental

of self-knowledge that she understands and gains new appreciation
of all the great truths concerning God and humanity that nourish her
faith.

Self-knowledge, in the sense in which Catherine uses the term, is
not a morbid introspection, nor is it merely a psychological self-understanding. It is rather a knowledge of self which we gain by looking
at ourselves in the light of the one who created us. This does not mean
that Catherine is not concerned with true self-knowledge, but rather
that she realizes that, although we can come so far in understanding
ourselves by looking at ourselves, we can never arrive at the deepest,
richest self-understanding without seeing ourselves through God's
eyes, or as she puts it, without gazing at ourselves in the "gentle
mirror" of God.[16] The reason that we can see ourselves in God is that
we are made in the divine image. The type of self-knowledge of which
Catherine speaks can perhaps be described as theological self-knowledge.

Self-knowledge is really a double knowledge: it is a knowledge of
ourselves acquired by looking at God, and a knowledge of God
acquired by reflecting on God's goodness toward us. Catherine explains this double knowledge well:

> As the soul comes to know herself she also knows God
> better, for she sees how good he has been to her. (D 13)

Besides referring to self-knowledge as a cell to which she with-
draws, Catherine also refers to it as a house in which one is at home
with oneself and with one's God, and to a well at the bottom of which
one finds the living, bubbling water of God's infinite being within
oneself.[17]

Through self-knowledge we come to appreciate both our dignity

---

maxim" of Catherine's spiritual life (cf. *Life* I, 10, 92-96). This opinion is
subscribed to by many catherinian scholars, including G. Cavallini, R.
Garrigou-Lagrange, K. Foster, A. Grion and G. D'Urso. Raymond of
Capua attributes Catherine's emphasis on self-knowledge to a prayer
experience which she had early on in her life in which Jesus Christ said
to her: "Do you know, daughter, who you are and who I am? . . . You are
the one who is not, whereas I am the one who is" (*Life* I, 10, 92).

16. Catherine likes the image of God the mirror to explain how we can best
come to know ourselves (cf. D 13, 167). It is interesting that she sees God
not as a "harsh" but as a "gentle" mirror.

17. Cf. L 26, L 154, and D 73 for the image of the house; and L 41 (DT III) for
the image of the well.

and our "nothingness." Catherine asks us to hold together both these perspectives on ourselves for we need them in order to know who we are and who God is. Our dignity comes from the fact that we are created in the image of the Trinity, participate in God's beauty, are redeemed by Jesus Christ and are destined for an eternal life of communion with God. Catherine is told:

> It was with providence that I created you, and when I contemplated my creature in myself I fell in love with the beauty of my creation. . . . All this my gentle providence did, only that you might be capable of understanding and enjoying me and rejoicing in my goodness by seeing me eternally. (D 135)

Our smallness comes from the fact that, as creatures, we are limited, incomplete and inadequate of ourselves, and that as sinners, we are capable of thwarting God's plan.

One of Catherine's emphases in her writings is that love follows knowledge, meaning that we need to know in order to love.[18] So, as we grow in knowledge of ourselves and of God, we also grow in our ability to love God and others. In the *Dialogue*, God tells Catherine that one moves "from the knowledge of me to the knowledge of oneself, from love of me to love of one's neighbors" (D 11). However, while knowledge leads to love, love, in its turn, leads to greater knowledge. Significantly, at the end of the *Dialogue*, Catherine, who all through the book has been progressively given more knowledge in order that she may love better, asks once again for knowledge: "Clothe, clothe me with yourself eternal Truth" (D 167). Knowledge and love are in Catherine's experience and understanding inseparable and mutually enriching, knowledge being joined to love "like an engrafted shoot" (D 9).

Style and Language

Catherine of Siena's style of writing is spontaneous, energetic and passionate. Much of its vitality comes from her superb use of imagery.

---

18. Cf. D 1. G. Cavallini notes that the thread running through all her teaching is "truth fostering love" (cf. Cavallini's "Introduzione" to *Il Dialogo*, xxvii-xxix).

Generally speaking, mystics, like poets, cannot express themselves without symbol or image. Catherine the mystic, in attempting to communicate her inexpressible experience of the most profound realities, relies on images to stimulate the dormant intuition of her readers, and to open for them the deeper meaning of human and divine truths. In her writings, metaphor trips over metaphor, and one barely-formed image gives way to another. It is as if she can never find words or images to adequately communicate what she knows and has experienced.

Catherine's language is distinctly her own. This is particularly evident in the anthropomorphic terms she uses to speak of God. Her God is "mad with love" and "drunk with love," and acts "as if he cannot live without us." While her anthropomorphism, like her imagery, is a testimony to the inadequacy of human language to speak about the divine, it is also an expression of her own lively faith in a personal God, full of love and mercy.

John Paul II, in his Apostolic Letter to mark the beginning of the new millennium, refers to the "lived theology" of the saints.[19] He suggests that, in the face of the mystery of human existence with its deep joy and profound suffering, the "lived theology" of the saints can offer us "precious insights which enable us to understand more easily the intuition of faith." Catherine of Siena is one of the three saints singled out by the pope as having a lived theology. The phrase "lived theology" gets to the core of what she offers us in her teaching. In Catherine's own time, a noted theologian who knew her well, made the same point when he remarked that she was able to taste the "inner fruit," rather than being content with the "outer rind," of spiritual truths.[20]

It is hoped that the selection of passages from her writings found in the following pages will bring Catherine's "lived theology" to life inviting us to enjoy the fruit, and not just be content with the outer rind, of our Christian faith.

Mary O'Driscoll, O.P.

---

19. *Novo Millennio Ineunte* 27, AAS 2001. English edition in Catholic Truth Society, "At the Beginning of the New Millennium", 2002.
20. From the "Processo Castellano," quoted in A. Levasti, *My Servant Catherine*, London, Blackfriars, 1954, p. 81.

Catherine of Siena

Spiritual Writings

Letters

Catherine of Siena was a prodigious letter-writer. Indeed, letter-writing can be considered as one of her most important forms of apostolic activity. Almost four hundred of her letters have been handed down to us. When we look at an index of the persons to whom she wrote we realize how wide and varied her correspondence was. There are letters addressed to members of her family, including her mother, brothers and a niece; to her friends, among them a poet, an artist, a lawyer, a craftsman and a widow; to public figures, for example, popes, bishops, a king, a queen and rulers of various Italian states; and to many other people: among them nuns, hermits, a prostitute, and a mercenary soldier. Her correspondents represent the famous, the infamous, and the ordinary woman and man.

Even a cursory perusal of Catherine's letters brings to our notice the personal touch of each letter. Each is obviously written to a particular person whom she meets wherever he or she is, with his or her particular joys and sorrows, problems and concerns, strengths and weaknesses, and specific circumstances in life. It is evident that Catherine delights in the uniqueness of each person. She displays delicate sensitivity and good common sense as she deals with the different temperaments, needs and situations of one correspondent after another. Besides their spiritual value, the letters are important in that they provide interesting autobiographical and historical facts. Considered as literature, they rank Catherine among the great Italian letter-writers of the fourteenth century.

The secret of Catherine's ability to meet different persons where they are in life, and to write words that are helpful to each, lies in her exceedingly deep, compassionate love for each person with whom she corresponds. Her greeting, "dearest" or "dear" at the beginning of each letter is therefore no empty formula. The same can be said about her standard opening and closing phrases, "In the name of Jesus Christ crucified and of gentle Mary" ... "Remain in the holy and gentle love of God," both of which indicate the faith atmosphere in which she lived, as well as her utter confidence in God's love and the power of Christ's passion.

Through her letter-writing, Catherine of Siena found a way to bring together her love of God and her love of neighbor, for it is obvious that the love she communicates to others in her letters is an overflow of the love which she herself receives in her own prayerful relationship with God.

In coming to an appreciation of Catherine of Siena's theology and spirituality, the letters are a good place to begin, for they, in contrast to the *Dialogue* which has a less familiar tone and can at times be diffuse and complicated, deal succinctly with one or two topics, and have immediate human appeal.

The letters of Catherine of Siena are contained in six volumes: *Le Lettere di S. Caterina da Siena*, edited by Piero Misciattelli, with notes by Niccolò Tommaseo. There is also a critical edition of 88 letters, *Epistolario di Santa Caterina da Siena*, edited by Eugenio Dupré Theseider. The passages from the letters which appear on the following pages have been translated by the editor of this present work from both these sources. The reference to a specific letter is indicated by L followed by the relevant number in the Misciattelli-Tommaseo edition. If the letter is also found in Dupre Theseider, this is indicated by DT followed by the relevant number. To date, there is no complete English translation of the letters but there are two editions of selected letters: *I, Catherine*, edited by Kenelm Foster and Mary John Ronayne; and *The Letters of St. Catherine of Siena*, edited by Suzanne Noffke.

Bear All Your Troubles Patiently

From a letter to Catherine's eldest brother, Benincasa, when he was living in Florence and had many financial difficulties.

In the name of Jesus Christ crucified and of gentle Mary.

Dearest brother in Christ Jesus,

I Catherine, a useless servant, comfort and bless you, and I invite you to a gentle, holy patience, without which we cannot please God. I beg you, therefore, to hold the weapon of patience firmly so that you may receive benefit from all your troubles. If it seems very difficult for you to cope with your many trials, there are three things which I suggest may help you to endure more patiently. Firstly, I want you to think about the shortness of life, for you are not certain even of tomorrow. We can indeed say that we do not have our past troubles, nor those which are in the future; all we have is the moment of time in which we are now. Surely then we ought to endure patiently since time is short.

Secondly, consider the benefit we gain from our troubles, for Saint Paul says that there is no comparison between our difficulties and the fruit and reward of eternal glory (cf. Rom 8:18). Thirdly, reflect on the evil consequences of indulging in anger and impatience. These evil consequences are with us both here and hereafter. So I beg you dearest brother to bear all your troubles patiently. . . .

Remain in the holy, gentle love of God. Gentle Jesus, Jesus love.

(L 18; DT XIV)

Prayer Is of Three Kinds

From a letter to Catherine's niece, Sister Eugenia, a nun at the monastery
of St. Agnes, at Montepulciano near Siena.

In the name of Jesus Christ crucified and of gentle Mary.

Dearest daughter in Christ gentle Jesus,

I Catherine, servant and slave of the servants of Jesus Christ, write
to you in his precious blood with desire to see you tasting the food of
angels, for you have been created for nothing else. In order that you
might taste it, God redeemed you with the blood of his only-begotten
Son. Reflect, dearest daughter, that this food is not eaten on earth, but
above; therefore the Son of God chose to be lifted up on the wood of
the holy cross so that we might receive this food at this table on high.
But you may ask me: "What is this food of angels?" My answer is that
it is the desire of God which draws to itself the desire that is in the
depths of the soul, in such a way that together they make one thing. . . .

Prayer is of three kinds. The first is unceasing: it is a holy constant
desire which prays in the sight of God, no matter what you are doing.
This desire directs all your activities, spiritual and corporal, to God's
honor, and so it is described as unceasing. The glorious saint Paul
seemed to be referring to this when he urged: "Pray constantly" (1
Thes 5:17). The second kind is vocal prayer: you engage in this when
you say the office or other prayers aloud. This is meant to bring you
to the third kind, namely, mental prayer. Your soul reaches this kind
of prayer through the use of vocal prayer with prudence and humility,
so that while the tongue speaks, the heart is not far from God.
However, you need to try hard to hold and keep your heart in the
power of God's love. And whenever you perceive that God is visiting
your mind so that it is drawn in any way to think of its Creator, you
ought to abandon vocal prayer and to fix your mind with great love
on God's visitation. Then when this ends, if there is time, you ought
to take up vocal prayer again so that the mind may always be full
rather than empty.

If you encounter different kinds of struggle in your prayer, or if
you experience confusing darkness of mind (this is the devil making

the soul feel that her prayer is not pleasing to God), you ought, nevertheless, never give up on account of struggles and darkness, but rather to stand firm with courage and perseverance, remembering that the devil does this to draw you away from your mother, prayer, and that God permits it to test the courage and constancy of your soul. God allows this also so that in your struggle and darkness you may know that of yourself you are nothing, and may know, through the good intention in which you remain, the goodness of God who is the giver and the preserver of a good and holy will. A will such as this is not granted to everyone who desires it.

By this means, the soul reaches the third and last kind of prayer, namely, mental prayer in which she receives the reward of the trials she experienced in her imperfect vocal prayer. She then tastes the milk of faithful prayer. She rises above herself, that is, above the gross impulses of the senses, and with angelic mind is united with God in intense love. By the light of her intellect she sees and knows, and she clothes herself with truth, becoming the sister of the angels. She abides with her bridegroom at the table of crucified desire, rejoicing to seek the honor of God and the salvation of souls, for she sees clearly that this eternal bridegroom ran to the shameful death of the cross, in obedience to the Father and for our salvation. This prayer is surely a mother who by the love of God conceives virtues, and who brings them to birth in love of neighbor. . . .

The soul receives and tastes this mother, prayer, more or less perfectly, according as she nourishes herself with the food of angels, that is, with a holy and true desire for God, raising herself up, as I said, to receive it at the table of the most gentle cross. That is why I told you that I desired to see you nourished with angelic food, for I do not see how otherwise you can be a true bride of Christ crucified, consecrated to him in holy religion. Do your best to be a precious jewel in God's sight. Bathe and drown yourself in the gentle blood of your bridegroom.

I have nothing more to say. Remain in the holy, gentle love of God. Gentle Jesus, Jesus love.

(L 26)

Let Us Plunge Into the Well

From a letter to the Dominican friar, Thomas della Fonte, Catherine's cousin and her first confessor.

In the name of Jesus Christ crucified.

Dearest and very loved father of our souls in Christ Jesus,

Catherine, Alessa and all your other daughters commend ourselves to you, desiring to see you well in body and soul, according to God's will. . . .

Dearest father, I beg you to fulfill my desire, which is to see you united to, and transformed into God. However, we cannot reach this point unless we are united with God's will. O sweet, eternal will, you have taught us the way to discover your will! And if, most merciful Father, we were to ask your gentle, loving Son about this way, he would answer as follows: "Dearest children, if you want to discover and know the fruit of my will, dwell always in the cell of your soul." This cell is a well containing soil as our own poverty, knowing that of ourselves we are nothing. In this knowledge we appreciate that our very existence comes to us from God.

O indescribable and blazing charity, I see that when we have found the soil, we also discover the living water,[1] namely, true knowledge of his sweet and holy will that desires nothing other than our sanctification (cf. 1 Thes 4:3). Let us then plunge into this deep well. When we are there, we shall know ourselves and we shall also know God's goodness. Recognizing that we are nothing of ourselves, we are humbled, and so we are able to enter into the blazing, fiery, open heart [of Christ], which like an unfastened window is never closed. When we gaze at it with the eye of free will which God has given us, we see clearly that his will is only for our sanctification. Love, sweet love, open, open our memory to receive and hold God's tremendous goodness, and to understand it, for through understanding we love, and through loving we are united and transformed in the love that is the

---

1. Catherine is probably thinking of the process of making a new well, in which layers of soil have to be dug through before the running water below is found.

mother of charity, having passed through, and yet never ceasing to pass through the door which is Christ crucified who promised his disciples: "I will come and make my home with you" (Jn 14:23).

This is my desire: to see you in this home, fully transformed. I want this for you in particular, and also for everyone else. I beg you to remain fastened and nailed to the cross. . . .

Catherine, servant and slave redeemed with the blood of the Son of God.

Forgive me for any presumptuous word I have said. May God set you on fire with love. Gentle Jesus, gentle Jesus, Jesus, gentle Jesus.

(L 41; DT IV)

Be a Vessel which You Fill at the Fountain

From a letter to Monna Alessa dei Saraceni, a young widow and a good friend of Catherine, who like her was a Dominican laywoman belonging to the Mantellate.

In the name of Jesus Christ crucified and of gentle Mary.

Dearest daughter in Christ, gentle Jesus,

I Catherine, servant and slave of the servants of Jesus Christ and your poor unworthy mother, want you to reach the perfection to which God has called you. . . .

Be a vessel which you fill and drink at the fountain.[2] Even though you draw your love from God who is the fountain of living water (cf. Jn 4:10; 7:37), if you do not drink it continually in him, your vessel will soon become empty. This is the sign that you are not drinking fully in God: if you suffer pain from the person you love, either because of a conversation you have had, or because you are deprived of some familiar consolation or because of some other accidental cause. If you

---

2. Catherine may be thinking of the large fountain at Fontebranda near her home where, when a container stands underneath the flow of water, water can be drawn continuously from it without its ever becoming empty.

suffer because of this, or because of anything else except an offense against God, it is a clear sign that your love is still imperfect, and that you have drawn away from the fountain.

In what way, then, can the imperfect be made perfect? This way: by correcting and chastising the movements of your heart with true self-knowledge, and with hatred and disgust for your imperfection, seeing that you are so discourteous as to give to the creature the love that ought to belong wholly to God, by loving the creature without moderation, while loving God moderately. For love of God should be measureless, and that for the creature should be measured against our love of God, and not by the measure of our own spiritual or temporal consolation. So then, do your best to love everyone in God, and to correct every inordinate affection.

Make two homes for yourself, my daughter. One will be your actual cell which will keep you from running all over the place, except when it is necessary, or in obedience to your prioress, or for the sake of charity. The other will be a spiritual home which you carry with you always, the cell of true self-knowledge where you find within yourself knowledge of God's goodness. This is actually two cells in one[3]: when you are in the one, you need to be in the other too, for otherwise you would fall into either confusion or presumption. For if you had only self-knowledge, you would experience confusion of mind; and if you had only knowledge of God, you would fall into presumption. The one therefore needs to be seasoned by the other, so that together they become one and the same thing. If you do this you will reach perfection. . . .

Remain in the holy, gentle love of God. Gentle Jesus, Jesus love.

(L 49)

---

3. Catherine always links self-knowledge with knowledge of God. One of her principal teachings is that it is only in knowing ourselves that we come to know God, and that only in knowing God do we come to know who and what we are. She sees this kind of self-knowledge as a cell in which we should dwell constantly.

Love Others Tenderly

This letter from Catherine was sent to Caterina di Scetto, a Dominican laywoman who belonged to the Mantellate in Siena.

In the name of Jesus Christ crucified and of gentle Mary.

Dearest sister and daughter in Christ gentle Jesus,

I Catherine, servant and slave of the servants of Jesus Christ, write to you in his precious blood, desiring to see you a true servant and bride of Christ crucified. We ought to be servants because we are bought with his blood. However, I do not see that we can be of any profit to him by our service. We ought then to be of profit to our neighbors because they are the means by which we test and gain virtue. You know that every virtue receives life from love, and love is gained in love, that is, by raising the eye of our intellect to consider how much we are loved by God. Seeing that we are loved, we cannot do anything except love. Loving God we embrace virtue out of love, and we despise vice out of hatred.

So you see that it is in God that we conceive virtues, and in our neighbors that we bring them to birth. You know indeed that you give birth to the child charity that is in your soul in order to answer your neighbor's need; and that you give birth to patience when your neighbor does you harm. You offer prayer for all your neighbors, and particularly for the one who has wronged you. That is the way we ought to behave; if others are unfaithful to us, we ought to be faithful to them, faithfully seeking their salvation and loving them gratuitously and not as a debt. In other words, take care not to love your neighbor for your own profit, for that would not be responding to the love which God has for you. For as God has loved you gratuitously so he wills that since you cannot love him in this way, you would do so toward your neighbors, loving them, as I said, gratuitously and not as a debt. You should neither diminish nor grudge your love toward others whether they offend you, or whether their love for you, or the joy or profit you gain from it, weakens. Rather, you should love them tenderly, accepting and putting up with their faults; and toward

God's servants you should have an attitude of gratitude and reverence.

Take care not to be like mad and foolish people who set themselves up to investigate and judge the deeds and habits of God's servants. Those who do this deserve severe correction. Reflect on this: to want to make all God's servants walk in our own way (which is impossible anyway) is no different from laying down laws and rules for the Holy Spirit. The person who is inclined to this kind of judgment needs to realize that the root of pride has not yet been plucked out, nor has true charity toward others (that is, a love that is given gratuitously and not as a debt) been implanted. Let us then love God's servants and not judge them. It is fitting for us to love all people in general, and to love those who are out of grace, with grief and bitterness over their sin because they offend God and their own souls. In this way you will be like gentle, loving Paul who weeps with those who weep, and rejoices with those who rejoice (cf. Rom 12:15). So, you will be sad with those who are in a pitiful state, through your desire for God's honor and their salvation, and you will rejoice with God's servants who are happy because they are united to God in deep love.

You see then that in our love of God we conceive virtues, and in our love of neighbor they are brought to birth. Acting in this way— loving your neighbor sincerely without false love or pretence of heart, without any thought of your own profit, spiritual or temporal—you will be a true servant, and respond by means of your neighbor to the love which your Creator has for you. . . .

Remain in the holy, gentle love of God. Gentle Jesus, Jesus, love.

(L 50)

There Is a Time to Be Together
and a Time to Be Separated

Catherine wrote this letter from Rocca di Tentennano (also called Rocca
d'Orcia, because it is in the valley of the river Orcia), south of Siena,
where she and several others, laypersons and priests, were involved in
a mission of preaching and reconciliation. Evidently, her two address-
ees, Caterina of the Hospital and Giovanna di Capo, whom she had left
in charge of her spiritual family in Siena, had complained about her
long absence.

In the name of Jesus Christ crucified and of gentle Mary.

Dearest daughters in Christ gentle Jesus,

I Catherine, servant and slave of the servants of Jesus Christ, write
to you in his precious blood, desiring to see you obedient daughters
united in true and perfect charity. Obedience and love enable you to
overcome every suffering and darkness. Obedience takes away the
thing that causes us pain, namely, our own perverse will (which is
denied and removed in true holy obedience), and darkness is scat-
tered and dissolved by the power of love and unity, for God is true
charity and highest eternal light. Those who have this true light as
their guide cannot lose their way (cf. Jn 14:6). Therefore, dearest
daughters, since it is so necessary, I want you to try to lose your own
wills and to gain this light.

This is the doctrine which, I remember, you have always been
taught, although you have learned little of it. I beg you then, dearest
daughters, to do what you haven't yet done. If you don't, you will
find yourselves suffering continually, and you will pull me (who am
deserving of all suffering) down too.

It is fitting that we should do for the honor of God what the holy
apostles did. When they had received the Holy Spirit, they separated
from one another, and from that gentle mother Mary. We can surmise
that their greatest joy was to be together, yet they gave up this joy in
order to seek the honor of God and the salvation of souls. And
although Mary sent them forth, they did not think that her love had
diminished, or that they were deprived of her concern for them in any
way. This is the rule we must follow.

I know that my presence is a great consolation to you, but, for God's honor and the salvation of souls, being truly obedient you will not seek your own consolation. Do not give advantage to the devil who wants to make you believe that you have lost the love and concern that I have for your souls and your bodies. If this were the case, it would not be true love. Let me assure you that it is in God alone that I love you. Why then do you feel such unreasonable pain about something that cannot be helped? Indeed, how shall we fare when big things have to be done if we are so weak in little ones? According to circumstances, we need to be able to be together or to be separated from one another. Right now, our gentle Savior wills and permits that for his honor we should be separated.

You are in Siena; Cecca and grandmother are in Montepulciano; fra Bartolomeo and fra Matteo have either gone to Siena or are going there; Alessa and Monna Bruna are at Monte Giove, eighteen miles from Montepulciano where they are staying with the countess and Donna Isa. Fra Raymond, fra Thomas, Monna Tomma, Lisa and I are all here at Rocca among scoundrels. There are so many incarnate devils to eat that fra Thomas says he has a stomach-ache![4] Yet they cannot be satisfied with this but are hungry for more, and are being well rewarded for all their work. Pray God in his goodness to give them big morsels, both sweet and bitter! Think how God's honor and the salvation of souls is being gently manifested! You should not want or desire anything else. You can do nothing more pleasing to God's supreme eternal will and to mine. Courage, my daughters; make the sacrifice of your wills to God. Don't keep crying for babies' milk when, as necessity requires, you ought to be chewing hard tough bread with the teeth of desire.

I have no more to say. Let yourselves be bound with the gentle bond of love. In this way, and no other, will you be daughters. Get your strength in Christ gentle Jesus, and strengthen all the others too. We shall return as soon as possible, according as it pleases God's goodness. Remain in the holy gentle love of God. Gentle Jesus, Jesus love.

(L 118)

---

4. In her writings, Catherine often uses the metaphor of "eating souls" to speak about winning people over to Christ.

Behave Like a Person in Love

Catherine sent this letter from Pisa to the Dominican friar, Bartolomeo Dominici, who was her confessor for a time.

In the name of Jesus Christ who was crucified for us.

Most beloved and dearest father (out of reverence for the most blessed sacrament)[5] and son in Christ Jesus,

I Catherine, servant and slave of the servants of Jesus Christ, write to you, sending comfort through his precious blood, and desiring to see you burning and consumed in his blazing love. I know that those who are burning and consumed in this love are not centered on themselves, and that's the way I want you to be.

I invite you to plunge through this burning love into the deep, peaceful sea. I have just discovered this again—not that the sea is new, but that it is new to me[6] in the feeling of my soul—in the phrase, "God is love" (1 Jn 4:8). And in this phrase, as a mirror reflects a person's face, and as the sun reflects its light on the earth, so this phrase reflects in my soul that all God's works, whatsoever they are, are love alone, for they are not the result of anything except love. For this reason, God says, "I am God Love." This sheds light on the unfathomable mystery of the incarnate Word who out of pure love was given to us in such humility that my pride is shamed. It teaches us not to look only at his deeds, but also at the blazing love which is the gift of this Word to us. It tells us that we are to behave like a person in love who, when a friend comes with a gift does not look at the gift in the friend's hands, but rather opens the eye of love and gazes at the friend's heart and affection. That is the way God wants us to act when the supreme, eternal, gentlest goodness of God visits our soul.

When God visits you with measureless gifts, let your memory open immediately to receive what your intellect knows in his divine love, and let your will rise with burning desire to receive and gaze at the

---

5. Catherine had extraordinary respect for those who consecrated the eucharistic elements.
6. It is possible that when she went to Pisa Catherine saw the sea for the first time.

blazing heart of the giver, the gentle, good Jesus.[7] Thus you will find yourself burning and clothed with fire, and with the gift of the blood of God's Son, and you will be free from all pain and unease. This is what took away the pain of the holy disciples when they had to leave Mary and one another, although they willingly bore the separation in order to spread the word of God. Run, run, run.

I cannot answer you concerning Benincasa's affairs as I am not in Siena. Thank Messer Nicolao for his kindness toward them. . . . May God be always in your soul. Amen, Jesus, Jesus.

Catherine, servant of the servants of God.

(L 146; DT XXVII)

Act Your Age!

From a letter to Monna Colomba, an elderly widow who lived in Lucca. Apparently Colomba was living a frivolous, superficial life, much caught up in seeking pleasure and trying to please her upper-bracket relatives. The worst aspect of her life seems to have been her seducing of younger women into following her example.

In the name of Jesus Christ crucified and of gentle Mary,

Dearest sister and daughter in Christ gentle Jesus,

I Catherine, servant and slave of the servants of Jesus Christ, write to you in his precious blood, desiring to see you a fruitful field which receives the seed of God's word and so bears fruit for yourself and for others. You are already becoming an old woman and are free of worldly ties, and so I want you to be a mirror of virtue to young women who are still tied to the world through their husbands.

Alas, sadly I realize that we are unfruitful ground, for we let God's word be smothered by the thorns and brambles of disordered affections and worldly desires, following the way of luxury and pleasure

---

7. Catherine, following Augustine (*De Trinitate* X, 11), refers here to the three powers of the soul, memory, intellect and will, by which we are in the image of the Trinity. She shows how all three powers are involved in our prayer.

and doing our best to be pleasing to creatures rather than to our Creator.[8] And there is a worse tragedy still: not satisfied with doing harm to ourselves, we also present ourselves as examples of sin and vanity to others for whom we should be models of virtue and integrity. Just as the devil did not want to fall alone but rather to bring many companions with him, so, it seems, we want to attract others to those same vanities and amusements that we indulge in ourselves.

You should withdraw, out of love of virtue and salvation, from vain frivolities and worldly weddings (for they are not in keeping with your state in life), and also try to discourage others who are inclined to these things. Instead of doing that, however, you speak wickedly, seducing young women who, through love of virtue, want to keep away from these things because they see that they offend God. I am not surprised, then, that no fruit appears, since, as I mentioned, the seed has been smothered.

Maybe you want to latch on to some excuse like, "I need to give in to my friends and relatives by acting like this; otherwise they will be upset and annoyed with me." So fear and perverted self-indulgence drain us of life, and many times even bring death, stealing from us the perfection which God has chosen for us and calls us to. This excuse is not acceptable to God for we should not give in to others in any matter that offends God and our own soul; nor should we love and serve others except in ways that are of God and are in keeping with our state in life.

Alas (miserable wretch that I am), did our relatives or friends or anyone else redeem us? No; Christ crucified alone was the Lamb who with unfathomable love offered his body to be sacrificed, giving us himself as bath and medicine, food and clothing, and as a bed in which we can rest.[9]

God cannot free you from the world when you are smothered and suffocated by your worldly affections and disordered desires. Come now, have you more than one soul? No. If you had two, you could give one to God and the other to the world. And you haven't more

---

8. Notice how Catherine here, in her desire to reach Colomba, identifies with her by using the first-person plural.

9. In several places in her writings, Catherine refers to God, to Christ and to the Holy Spirit as our "bed," thereby indicating that God is the one who can support and refresh us, and give us rest, no matter how tired or heavily burdened we feel.

than one body either, and yet you are fritting away its energy on all kinds of silly things.

Give to the poor from your material possessions. Submit to the yoke of holy, true obedience. Deny, deny your will in such a way that it is not tied to your relatives. Mortify your body instead of delicately pampering it. Despise yourself, and do not pay attention to social standing or wealth, for virtue is the only thing that makes us noble, and the riches of this life indicate the worst kind of poverty when they are possessed with inordinate love keeping us away from God. . . .

Hurry, hurry, for time is short and the road is long. Even if you offered all you possess in the world, time would not wait for you but would keep on running its course. I have no more to say. Remain in the holy gentle love of God. Forgive me if I have said too much; the love and concern which I have for your salvation have made me do so. Please understand that I would rather *do* something for you instead of just talking. May God fill you with his gentle grace. Gentle Jesus, Jesus love.

(L 166)

Do Not Fast Unless You Are Able

In this letter sent to Monna Agnese, wife of the tailor, Francesco, who lived in Florence, Catherine gives simple, sensible advice on how to live the Christian life.

In the name of Jesus Christ crucified and of gentle Mary.

Dearest daughter in Christ gentle Jesus,

I Catherine, servant and slave of the servants of Jesus Christ, write to you in his precious blood, desiring to see you clothed in true and perfect humility, for this is a little virtue that makes us great in the gentle sight of God. It is the virtue which compelled and inclined God to make his most gentle Son incarnate in Mary's womb. It is as exalted as the proud are humbled; it shines in the sight of God and of human beings; it binds the hands of the wicked. It unites the soul to God; it purifies and washes away the dross of sin; and it cries out to God for mercy. Dearest daughter, I want you to possess this wonderful virtue so that you can pass over the tempestuous sea of this world free from storms and danger.

Strengthen yourself with this gentle, true virtue, and bathe yourself in the blood of Christ crucified. When you can find the time for prayer, I beg you to use it. And love everyone tenderly. I ask and command you not to fast except on the days laid down by holy Church, if you are able. But if you do not feel strong enough to fast, then don't do so. At other times, do not fast except on Saturdays if you are able. When this intense heat is over, fast on the feasts of holy Mary, if you can, but no more than that. Drink something besides water every day. Try hard to increase your holy desire, and don't bother about other things.

Do not be anxious or depressed about us, for we are all well. When it pleases God's goodness we shall see one another again. That's all I have to say. Remain in the holy, gentle love of God. Comfort my dear daughters, Ursula and Genevieve. Gentle Jesus, Jesus love.

(L 174)

Look at Yourself in the Water

A short passage, connecting knowledge of God's love for us with our love for others, from a long letter to Raymond of Capua when he was living in Rome. Catherine believed it was through Mary's care of her that Raymond came into her life as her confessor, friend and adviser.

In the name of Jesus Christ crucified and of gentle Mary.

Dearest and beloved father and son in Christ Jesus, given to me by our gentle mother Mary,

I Catherine, servant and slave of the servants of Jesus Christ, write to you in his precious blood, desiring to see you true sons and preachers[10] of the incarnate Word, the Son of God, not only in your

---

10. Use of the plural suggests that, although the letter is addressed to

words, but also in your actions. You will learn this from the master of
truth, who first practiced virtue and then preached it. In this way you
will bear fruit and will be channels through which God will pour
grace into the hearts of your hearers. . . .

When a soul is not selfishly self-regarding, but considers herself in
God, and God in God, because he is supreme eternal goodness worthy
of all our love—contemplating in God the effect of his burning,
consuming love—she finds in him the creature's image, and in that
image, which is herself, she finds God. In other words, the love a soul
sees that God has for her, she in turn extends to all creatures. She
immediately feels compelled to love her neighbor as herself for she
sees how fully she herself is loved by God when she beholds herself
in her source, the sea of God's being. She then desires to love herself
in God and God in herself, like a person who, on looking into the
water, sees his or her own image there; and in this vision loves and
delights in self. Those who are wise will be moved to love the water
rather than themselves, for if they had not first seen themselves, they
could not have loved nor taken delight in themselves; nor could they
have removed the mark on their face revealed to them in the water.

Reflect on this, my dearest sons: we can see neither our own dignity
nor the defects which spoil the beauty of our soul, unless we look at
ourselves in the peaceful sea of God's being in which we are imaged.
That is the source we came from when God's wisdom created us in
the divine image and likeness. . . .

Remain in the holy, gentle love of God. Gentle Jesus, Jesus love.

(L 226)

Raymond, it was meant for all the Dominican friars living at S. Maria
Sopra Minerva in Rome.

Come Gently without Any Fear

In this letter to pope Gregory XI, Catherine urges him to return from Avignon to his episcopal see in Rome. Knowing that he is excessively timid, hesitant to do anything that will upset his cardinals, she gently persuades him to be braver. Her tone is sensitive and reassuring. One can almost see her pumping confidence and courage into this vacillating pope.

In the name of Jesus Christ crucified and of gentle Mary.

Dear reverend and blessed father in Christ gentle Jesus,

Your poor unworthy daughter Catherine, servant and slave of the servants of Jesus Christ, writes to you, comforting you in his sweet blood. I desire to see you free of any servile fear, for I am aware that the fearful person does not persevere in the strength of holy resolution and good desire. I have prayed and will continue to pray that the gentle good Jesus will take away from you all servile fear and leave only holy fear.[11]

May burning charity so fill you that you will be prevented from hearing the voices of incarnate devils, and from paying attention to the advice of evil counsellors whose motivation is self-centered love. I hear that these people are trying to frighten you, saying you will be killed, in order to prevent your return.[12] I, however, on behalf of Christ crucified, tell you, dear holy father, not to be afraid for any reason whatever.

Come securely, trusting in Christ gentle Jesus, for if you do what is right, God will be on your side and nobody will be against you (cf. Rom 8:31). Father, get up courageously, because, I tell you, there is nothing to fear! However, if you don't do what you should, you will have every reason to be afraid. You ought to come. Come, come then gently, without any fear. And if any of those around you want to stop you, say to them fiercely, as Christ said, turning to Peter who out of

---

11. Here Catherine contrasts servile fear which is focused on self with holy fear which is focused on God and God's will.

12. Rumors were being circulated that the pope would be murdered if he set foot in Italy.

kindness wished to pull him back from going to his passion: "Get behind me, Satan! You are an obstacle in my path, because you are thinking not as God thinks but as human beings do. Do you not want me to do my Father's will?" (Mt 16:23). Do the same, dearest father; follow him whose vicar you are, deliberating and deciding for yourself, and saying in the presence of all who oppose you: "Even if I should lose my life a thousand times, I want to do the will of my eternal Father." (Accepting that your life will not be taken, you are still grasping the way and the means of continually gaining the life of grace.) So, have courage, and don't be unnecessarily afraid. Take up the weapon of the most holy cross which is security and life for Christians. Let those who want to, say whatever they like: you hold firmly to your holy resolution.

My father, fra Raymond, asked me on your behalf to pray to God in order to discern whether there was any obstacle. I had already prayed about this, before and after holy communion, and I saw neither death nor any danger. The dangers come from those who advise you. Believe, and have confidence in Christ gentle Jesus. I hope that God will not spurn so many prayers, made with burning desire, with many tears and much sweat. Please forgive me, please forgive me. I have no more to say. Remain in the holy gentle love of God.

(L 233; DT LXXVI)

If You Want to Rule Well Practice Justice

In this letter to the authorities in Bologna Catherine gives sound advice, as applicable today as it was in the fourteenth century, on how rulers should exercise authority in the community.

In the name of Jesus Christ crucified and of gentle Mary.

Dearest brothers in Christ gentle Jesus,

I Catherine, servant and slave of the servants of Jesus Christ, write to you in his precious blood, desiring to see you divested of the old self, and clothed in the new self (cf. Eph 4:24; Col 3:10). In other words,

I want to see you divested of the world and of sensual self-love, which is the ancient sin of Adam, and clothed with the new Christ gentle Jesus, that is, with his loving charity. When this charity is in the soul, she does not seek her own interests but is liberal and generous in returning what she owes to God, namely, love of him above everything else, and, hating and despising selfish pleasure-seeking, love of herself in God, giving glory and praise to his name; and what she owes to her neighbor, namely, good will rooted in tender charity and an ordered love. . . .

When one is in charge, one [often] fails in true justice. And this is the reason: one is afraid of losing one's status, so, in order not to displease others, one keeps covering and hiding their wrong-doing, smearing ointment on a wound which at the time needs to be cauterized. Alas, how sad I feel when those who should use the flame of divine charity to burn out crime by holy punishment and correction, administered in true justice, flatter others and pretend not to see their wrong-doing. They behave in this way toward those whom they think may harm their position. But toward the poor who seem insignificant and whom they do not fear, they display tremendous enthusiasm for "justice," and, showing neither mercy nor compassion, they exact harsh punishments for small faults.

What is the reason for such injustice? Self-centered love. Such miserable worldly people are deprived of truth, and therefore they do not recognize the truth—neither God's truth which desires their salvation nor their own truth which would keep them in a true position of lordship. If they knew the truth, they would see that only living in the fear of God preserves their position and the city in peace. In order to remain in true holy justice, rendering to all their subjects their due, they need to show mercy to those who deserve mercy, not on sudden impulse but out of truthful conviction. They need likewise to exercise justice toward those who deserve it, a justice seasoned with mercy and not the result of impulsive anger. Their motivation will be not what people say but holy true justice, and they will be concerned not for any private good but for the common good.

Their criterion in appointing officials and those who are to rule the city will not be partisanship or prejudice, not flattery or bribery, but only virtue and right reason. They will choose not immature boys, but good mature men who fear God, seeking the common good and not their own advantage. In this way, their position and their city will be preserved in peace and unity. But injustices, partisanship and the appointment as rulers and governors of those who do not know how to control themselves or their families—people who are unjust, hotheaded, impulsively angry and lovers of only themselves—these are the means by which they will lose their spiritual state of grace and their temporal status. One can quote to such as these: "If God does not guard the city, you labor in vain to guard it" (Ps 126:1) (meaning that you need to fear God and to keep him before you in your activity).

You understand, therefore, dearest brothers and lords, how self-centered love destroys the city of the soul, and also destroys and overturns our earthly cities. I want you to know that nothing has so divided the world, turning people against one another, as has self-centered love, from which injustices have sprung and still spring. . . .

Remember, then, that if you are clothed in sensual and selfish love, you cannot help God's servants, and that those who do not help themselves by growth in virtue and with enthusiasm for true justice, cannot help their people's city. I stress, therefore, that you need to be clothed in the new creature, Christ gentle Jesus, and his indescribable charity. But we cannot be so clothed unless we first divest ourselves— and I won't be able to divest myself unless I see how harmful it is to hold on to the old sin, and how useful is the new garment of divine charity. For when sin is seen, it is hated and stripped off; then a person loves, and in loving is clothed with the garment of virtue woven with the love of the new creature. This is the only way. That is why I told you that I desired to see you divested of the old self and clothed with the new self, Christ crucified. In this manner, you will gain and keep both the state of grace and the state of your city, and you will never fail in the reverence you owe to holy Church, but rather you will graciously render what you owe and keep your position of dignity.

I have no more to say. Remain in the holy gentle love of God. Gentle Jesus, Jesus love.

(L 268)

I Shall Wait For You at the Place of Execution

A letter to the Dominican, fra Raymond of Capua, Catherine's confessor and dear friend, in which she tells, with great empathy and compassion, of her visit to a young man, Niccolò di Toldo, from Perugia, who, condemned to death, was in prison in Siena, and of her subsequent presence at his execution.

In the name of Jesus Christ crucified and of gentle Mary.

Most loved father and dearest son in Jesus Christ,

I Catherine, servant and slave of the servants of God, write and commend myself to you in the precious blood of the Son of God, desiring to see you plunged and drowned in that sweet blood, which is fused with the fire of his blazing love. . . .

Up, dearest father, and let us sleep no more, for I have news that will not let me rest. I have just taken a head into my hands and have been moved so deeply that my heart cannot grasp it, nor my tongue speak of it. No eye has seen, and no ear has heard of such a thing (cf. 1 Cor 2:9). . . .

I went to visit the man you know. He received such strength and consolation from my visit that he went to confession and prepared himself well. He asked me to promise, for the love of God, that I would be with him when the time of execution came. I promised and I kept my word. So, that morning before the bell rang, I went to him, and I was greatly consoled. I took him to Mass and he received holy communion, which he had never done before. His will was conformed and open to God's will; he had just one fear, namely, that he might not be strong enough when the moment came. God, in his overwhelming and burning goodness deceived him however, by giving him such love and affection for *me* in God, that he did not know how to be without *him*. He kept saying: "Stay with me and don't leave me; then I shall be fine, and I shall die content." He leaned his head on my breast and I sensed both tremendous joy and the fragrance of his blood, not separate from the fragrance of my own blood which I hope to shed for gentle Jesus, my bridegroom. As my own desires increased, and I felt his fear, I said: "Courage, my dear brother; we shall soon be at the wedding-feast. You will go there bathed in the sweet blood of God's Son, and in the sweet name of Jesus. Never forget this. I shall be waiting for you at the place of execution." Imagine this, my father and son: his heart lost all its fear, his face changed from sadness to joy, and he rejoiced and exulted, saying: "How have I received so much grace that my soul's delight will be waiting for me at the holy place of my execution?" (He had been given so much light that he could call the execution place "holy".) And he added: "I shall go joyfully and courageously, and it will seem like a thousand years until I get there, thinking that you will be there waiting for me." He said such beautiful things that your heart would almost burst at the goodness of God.

I waited for him at the place of execution, and as I waited, I kept praying in the presence of Mary and Catherine, virgin and martyr. Before he arrived, I lay down and stretched my neck on the block, and begged Mary for the grace I wanted, namely, that I might give him light and peace of heart at the moment of death, and then see him reach his goal. I was so overcome by the gentle assurance I received about this, that although a great crowd was there, I saw no one.

Then he arrived, like a meek lamb, and when he saw me he began to smile. He asked me to make the sign of the cross over him, so I blessed him and said: "Down to the wedding-feast, my gentle brother. You will soon be in everlasting life." He prostrated with great meekness, and I stretched out his neck and bent down to him, reminding him of the blood of the Lamb. His lips kept murmuring only "Jesus" and "Catherine," and he was still murmuring when I received his head into my hands, while my eyes were locked on the divine goodness, as I said: "I will."

Then I saw the God-man, as one sees the radiance of the sun. He stood ready to receive [Niccolò's] blood into his own; and the fire of holy desire, which was poured into and concealed in that soul by grace, was now received into the fire of his own divine charity. After he received the blood and the desire, he received the soul also, and plunged it into the store-house of his open side brimming with mercy. In this way, First Truth showed me that he was saved, not by any works, but only by God's grace and mercy. How unspeakably moving it was to see God's goodness; to see with what gentleness and love he awaited that soul—gazing at it with eyes of mercy—as it left the body and entered into his open side, bathed in its own blood which now had value through the blood of God's Son. When he was received in this way by our powerful God (who has the power to do it), the Son who is wisdom and incarnate Word gave him a share in the crucified love with which, in obedience to the Father, he himself bore his own painful and shameful death for the sake of all humanity, and the hands of the Holy Spirit sealed him within.

He, however, did such a beautiful thing, so beautiful that it would melt a thousand hearts (and that does not surprise me for he was already enjoying the divine sweetness): he turned back, in the same way as a bride who has reached her bridegroom's threshold looks back and bows her thanks to the one who accompanied her there.

When he was at rest, my soul rested in peace and quiet, so aware of the fragrance of blood that I could not remove the blood which had splashed onto me. Alas, wretch that I am, I can say no more. With great envy, I saw myself left behind.

It seems that the first stone is already in place. Therefore, do not be surprised if I impose on you my desire to see you plunging into the blood and the fire which flow from the side of God's Son. So, my dear sons, no more negligence, for the blood has begun to flow and to receive life.

(L 273; DT XXXI)

Renew the Church with Love

This is Catherine's first letter to the new pope, Urban VI, who succeeded Gregory XI in 1378. While Gregory was timid and disinclined to do anything that would upset his cardinals and bishops, Urban was so intent on Church reform that he didn't seem to mind whom he offended. In fact, he often acted in such a harsh and arrogant manner that he alienated the very people he wanted to help. Here Catherine encourages him in his desire for reform but also counsels compassionate sensitivity toward those under him.

In the name of Jesus Christ crucified and of gentle Mary.

Most holy and dearest father in Christ gentle Jesus,

I Catherine, servant and slave of the servants of Jesus Christ, write to you in his precious blood, desiring to see you rooted in true and perfect charity, so that like a good shepherd you may lay down your life for your sheep. Truly, holy father, only those who are rooted in charity, and therefore free from self-centered love, are ready to die for the love of God and the salvation of souls. Those whose love is self-centered are not ready to give their lives; and not only that, such people, it seems, are unwilling to bear even the least suffering for they are always fearful about themselves, not wanting to lose the life of their bodies nor any of their comforts. Consequently, whatever they do, they do imperfectly and corruptly, since the source of their actions is corrupt. Whatever their state, pastor or subject, they show little sign of virtue.

Pastors who are rooted in true charity, however, do not act like this; rather, all they do is good and perfect since the source of their actions is united and joined to perfect divine charity. Such persons do not fear either the devil or creatures, only their Creator. They do not heed the detractions of the world, embarrassment, insults, derogatory jokes, unfavorable comments from their subjects who, when they are reproved by their prelate, become offended and begin to criticize. . . .

Truly, most holy father, I do not see how this can be done well unless you renew the garden of [the Church] your bride, filling it with good strong plants; taking the trouble to choose a band of holy people who are virtuous and do not fear death. Do not look for persons of high birth, but rather for good pastors who will take tender care of their flocks. Create a college of good cardinals who will be strong supports, helping you, with God's grace, to carry the weight of your many burdens.

O how happy will I be when I see that which is hers given back to the bride of Christ, and those who nourish themselves at her breast not thinking of their own good, but of the glory and praise of God's name as they feed on the food of souls at the table of the holy cross. I have no doubt that if that happens, your lay subjects will correct themselves, for they will not be able to do otherwise, urged on by their pastors' teaching and upright lives. We are not meant to lie down and sleep, but courageously and without negligence, to do what we can, even to the point of death, for the glory and praise of God's name.

Then, I beg and urge you for the love of Christ crucified, and out of love for that blood of which you are the minister, not to delay in welcoming back mercifully those sheep who have left the fold[13] (on account of my sins, I believe). Soften their obduracy with kindness and holiness, offering them the benefit of belonging to the fold once more. If they do not ask for this with true and perfect humility, let your holiness supply for their weakness. Be content to take from the sick only as much as they can give. O dear, o dear, have pity on so many souls that are perishing. . . .

I hope, by the gentle goodness of God, that you will be filled with his burning charity. This will enable you to perceive how terrible is the loss of souls and how much you are obliged to love them. In perceiving this, you will grow in eagerness and concern to free them from the hands of the devil, and will seek to heal the mystic body of holy Church and the universal body of the Christian religion.[14] You will seek particularly to reconcile your children, winning them back with kindness and with only as much stern justice as they are able to take, and no more. I am convinced that this cannot be done without the virtue of charity. That is why I said that I wished to see you rooted in true and perfect charity. Not that I do not believe that you are in

---

13. This is a reference to the Tuscan cities that had rebelled against the pope. Catherine wrote this letter from Florence.

14. Catherine uses the term "mystic body" to refer to the pope and the ordained ministers in the Church (thereby indicating their special role at the eucharistic celebration), and the term "universal body" to refer to all the members of the Church.

charity, but because, as long as we are pilgrims and strangers in this life, we can grow in the perfection of charity. I said that I desired this perfection in you, and that it be nourished constantly with the fire of holy desire. In this way, like a good pastor, you will bring it to life in your subjects also. I implore you to do this. For my part, I shall continue until I die to work by prayer and by every other means for the honor of God and for your peace and that of your children.

I have no more to say to you. Remain in the holy gentle love of God. Forgive my presumption, holy father, but love and sorrow are my excuse before your holiness. I humbly ask your blessing. Gentle Jesus, Jesus love.

(L 291)

Come Out of Your Wood

This is a letter sent by Catherine in 1378, when the schism had just begun, to two Augustinian hermits, William Flete from England, and Anthony from France. Both of these were living in the woods at Lecceto, not far from Siena. The pope, Urban VI, feeling the need to have prayerful supporters nearby, had asked these hermits, as he had asked Catherine, to come to Rome. They (or at least William) had refused, on the grounds that they would lose peace and tranquillity if they had to leave their wood. Catherine is gently scathing as she makes the point that God is to be found everywhere, and that attachment to a place, even a peaceful place of prayer, is a poor substitute for attachment to God's will.

In the name of Jesus Christ crucified and of gentle Mary.

Dearest sons in Christ gentle Jesus,

I Catherine, servant and slave of the servants of Jesus Christ, write to you in his precious blood, desiring to see you letting go of yourselves in such a way that you do not seek peace or tranquillity anywhere except in Christ crucified, hungering at the table of the cross for the honor of God, the salvation of souls and the reform of holy Church. Today we see the Church in such need that to help it we must deny ourselves by coming out of our woods. Seeing that you can bear fruit in the Church, this is not the time for you to stand still or to say, "I won't have any peace." Now that God has given us the grace of providing holy Church with a good, just shepherd whose delight is God's servants whom he wishes to have near him, and who hopes to be able to purify the Church by uprooting vice and planting virtue without fear, we others ought to support him in his just and courageous behavior.

I shall recognize whether we have truly conceived love for the reform of holy Church, because if this is indeed the case, you will follow the will of God and his vicar by coming out of your wood and hurrying to enter the field of battle. If you do not do this, you will not be in harmony with God's will. Therefore, I beg you, for the love of Christ crucified, to accede promptly with no delay to the request which the Holy Father makes of you. Do not hesitate thinking you might not find a wood, for there are woods and forests here.[15] Arise, dearest sons. Do not sleep any more for it is time to watch. I have no more to say to you. Remain in the holy, gentle love of God. Gentle Jesus, Jesus love.

Rome, 15 December 1378.

(L 326)

---

15. In the vicinity of Rome, from where Catherine is writing, solitary places, although not as wooded as Lecceto, could be found.

The Special Faith and Love of Friendship

Part of a letter written to her dear friend, Raymond of Capua, shortly before she died. In it she shows the depth of her love for him, and explains that between friends there is a bond of special faith as well as of special love.

In the name of Jesus Christ crucified and of gentle Mary.

Dearest father in Christ gentle Jesus,

I Catherine, servant and slave of the servants of Jesus Christ, write to you in his precious blood, desiring to see in you the light of most holy faith that illuminates for us the way of truth. . . .

I beg you dearest father to pray earnestly that you and I together may drown ourselves in the blood of the humble Lamb. This will make us strong and faithful. We shall then feel the fire of divine love, and we shall, through its grace, become doers instead of undoers and spoilers. In this way we shall express our fidelity to God, and our trust in his help, rather than in our own or others' expertise.

With this same faith we shall love creatures, for just as love of neighbor results from love of God, so does faith, in general and in particular. In other words, just as our love for all people in general corresponds to a general faith, so a particular faith operates between those who love each other more closely,[16] as you and I do. For, beyond a general love, there is between us a very close and special love which expresses itself in faith. And it expresses itself in such a way that it can neither believe nor imagine that the other could want anything except our good. It believes that the other constantly seeks that good with great urgency in the sight of God and creatures, and is always trying to bring about the glory of God's name and the soul's good. It believes also that the other is always begging for divine help, so that when our burdens increase, our courage and perseverance may increase too. This faith carries the one who loves and it never decreases for any reason whatsoever, no matter what people say or how the devil tries to deceive, and no matter how great a distance separates

16. This idea of special faith between friends is found in Dante, *Inferno* XI, 63.

the two. If it were otherwise, it would be a sign that their love of God and neighbor was imperfect.

It seems, from what I have gathered from your letter,[17] that you are experiencing many different struggles and diverse thoughts, caused by the devil's deceit and by your own extreme sensitivity. You felt that your burden was too heavy for you to bear, and that you were not strong enough to be measured by my standards. Accordingly, you began to doubt whether my love and concern for you had decreased. But you did not realize, though you yourself showed this to be the case, that my love had increased while yours had diminished. I love you with the love with which I love myself and with a lively faith that what is lacking on your part will be made up for by God in his goodness. . . . So my love for you is greater than before, not less. . . .

I beg you to forgive anything I have said that is not to God's honor or is lacking in respect toward you. My love is my excuse. There is no more to be said. Remain in the gentle, holy love of God. Gentle Jesus, Jesus love.

(L 344)

---

17. The pope, Urban VI, at the time of the schism, had sent Raymond on a reconciling mission to the king of France, but Raymond's courage had failed when he got as far as Genoa and found that his life was in danger. He wrote to Catherine telling her of his reluctance to continue his journey.

Prayers

Twenty-six of Catherine of Siena's prayers have been preserved for us. With one possible exception, these are not prayers that she herself wrote or even dictated to others. Rather, they were transcribed by one or other of her followers who were present as she prayed aloud. All of these prayers belong to the last four years of her life. They impress us by their simplicity, their intense concentration on God who is repeatedly praised and thanked, and their constant desire for the salvation of others. They have a sound theological base, being rooted in the great truths of the Christian faith. It is interesting to note how the themes that run through the *Dialogue* and the *Letters* are taken up in the *Prayers* and made the subject of Catherine's conversation with God. In her *Prayers*, her theology becomes doxology.

As her *Prayers* make evident, Catherine of Siena was a great intercessor. In them we find her pleading with God passionately and urgently for mercy for all: the world, the Church, the pope, her friends and followers, all in need. It is obvious that she does not regard intercession as merely a passing prayer to God on behalf of one or other person in time of crisis, but rather as an expression of her deep loving permanent commitment both to God and to her neighbor. In Catherine's own life, the importance and intensity of her intercession increased according as her union with God and her concern for others increased. This observation tells us something very significant about the prayer of intercession in the Christian life, namely, that it is not, as is sometimes thought, a type of prayer beyond which one passes on the way to the heights of mystical prayer, as though intercession were for beginners and mysticism for those who are advanced in the spiritual life, but is rather a type of prayer which belongs most particularly to the life of contemplative union with God.

The critical edition of Catherine of Siena's prayers in Latin and Italian has been done by G. Cavallini: *Le Orazioni*. There is an edited English translation of this text by Suzanne Noffke: *The Prayers of Catherine of Siena*. It is the translation used in this latter work that has been adopted in the following pages. The relevant prayer is indicated by P followed by its number as given in the Noffke text.

You Fashioned Us After Yourself

Godhead!
Godhead!
Ineffable Godhead!
O supreme goodness
that for love alone made us in your image and likeness!
For when you created humankind
you did not say (as when you created the other creatures),
"Let it be made."
No, you said—O unutterable love!—
"Let us make humankind in our image and likeness,"
so that in this the whole Trinity might give assent together,
and in the powers of our soul
you fashioned us after the very Trinity,[1]
Godhead eternal.
To fashion us after yourself, eternal Father—
you who as Father hold and keep all things within yourself—
you gave us memory
to hold and keep what our understanding perceives and knows
of you, infinite goodness.
And in knowing,
our understanding shares in the wisdom
of your only-begotten Son.
You gave us our will, gentle clemency, Holy Spirit,
which like a hand reaches up
filled with your love
to take whatever our understanding knows
of your unutterable goodness;
and then this will,

---

1. To be in God's image is to have within us the three powers of memory, understanding and will. Through our memory we are in the likeness of the Father who in his power holds all things; through our understanding we are in the likeness of the Son who in his wisdom knows all things, through our will we are in the likeness of the Spirit who is clemency and love. This threefold image of the Trinity in human beings is stressed often by Catherine, following Augustine (cf. *De Trinitate* X, II).

this strong hand of love,
fills our memory and affection with you.

Thanks, thanks be to you, high eternal Godhead,
that you have shown us such great love
by fashioning us with these gracious powers in our soul:
understanding to know you;
memory to keep you in mind,
to hold you within ourselves;
will and love to love you more than anything else.
It is only reasonable
that I should love you, infinite goodness,
once I know you.
And so powerful is this love
that neither demon nor anyone else can take it away from us
unless we so will.
How ashamed they should be, then,
who do not love you
though they see how much you have loved them!

(P 1)

Give Your Vicar a New Heart

Eternal goodness,
do not look at the wretched deeds we have committed
of our very own selves,
cutting ourselves off from your boundless goodness
and cutting our souls off from their proper goal.
No, I beg you,
in your infinite mercy
open the eye of your supreme clemency and compassion
and look at your one bride (cf. Eph 5:25-26).
Open the eye of your vicar on earth,[2]

---

2. The pope referred to here is Gregory XI who was still living in Avignon. Catherine, in her prayers as well as in her letters, shows an anxiety that this timid pope will have the courage to do what is right.

so that he may not love you for his own sake,
nor himself for his own sake,
but may love you for yourself and himself for your sake.
For when he loves either you or himself for his own sake
we are all lost,
because he who should be our life is our death
to the extent that he is not careful
to shelter us little sheep who are going astray.
But if he loves himself for your sake
and you for yourself,
we live,
because we receive our example for living
from the good shepherd.
Make him a new heart,
that he may constantly grow in grace
and be strong in raising the standard of the most holy cross
to make the unbelievers share as we do
in the fruit of the passion and blood
of your only-begotten Son,[3]
the spotless Lamb,
high, eternal, ineffable Godhead.
I have sinned against the Lord.
Have mercy on me!

(P 1)

You Are a Peaceful Sea

Godhead!
Godhead!
Eternal Godhead!
I proclaim and do not deny it:
you are a peaceful sea[4]

---

3. A reference to the Moslems who were taking over the Christian places in Palestine.
4. Catherine loves to call God the peaceful sea. Here she emphasizes, as she

in which the soul feeds and is nourished
as she rests in you
in love's affection and union
by conforming her will with your high eternal will—
that will which wants nothing other
than that we be made holy.
So the soul who considers this
strips herself of her own will
and clothes herself in yours.

O most gentle love,
it seems to me you are showing
that the truest sign people are dwelling in you
is that they follow your will
not in their own way
but in your way.
This is the surest sign that people are clothed in your will:
that they see the cause of events in your will
not in human will,
and that they rejoice
not in material prosperity
but in adversity,
which they see as given by your will
and motivated only by love.
So they love adversity
just as they love all the things you have created,
all of which are good and therefore worthy of love.
But sin is not from you
and is therefore not worthy of love.
And I, miserable wretch,
have sinned by loving sin.
I have sinned against the Lord.
Have mercy on me!

(P 2)

---

does in the *Dialogue* 79, that just as everything in a peaceful sea has no
movement except the gentle movement of the sea, so when we are totally
surrendered to God, the movement of God's will and our will is one.

Moved By Love You Sent Us Your Son

O Father all-powerful, eternal God,
O boundless most gentle charity!
I see in you
and know in my heart
that you are the way, truth, and life (cf. Jn 14:6)
by which everyone must travel
who is destined to come to you—
the way, truth, and life
which your unutterable love establishes and fashions
out of the true knowledge
of the wisdom
of your only-begotten Son, our Lord Jesus Christ.
You are the eternal and incomprehensible God
who, when the human race was dead
because of our wretched weakness,
were moved only by love
and by merciful compassion
to send us this one,
our true God and Lord,
Christ Jesus your Son,
clothed in our mortal flesh.
And it was your will that he should come
not with the pleasures and splendors of this passing world,
but in anxiety, poverty, and anguish,
knowing and accomplishing your will,
for our redemption counting as nothing
the world's perils and the enemy's obstructions
so that he might overcome death by dying,
being obedient even to the most bitter death of the cross.
Do not consider my wretchedness
as I pray to you for them,
but plant them in the garden of your will.
I bless you, O eternal Father,
that you may bless these servants of yours,[5]

---

5. Catherine is referring here to her friends and followers who were present
   with her as she prayed.

so that they may learn to reckon themselves
as nothing for your sake
and may follow your will,
which alone is purity,
which alone is eternal and everlasting.
And for all of them I give you thanks.
Amen.

(P 3)

I Plead with You for the World

Power of the eternal Father,
help me!
Wisdom of the Son,
enlighten the eye of my understanding!
Tender clemency of the Holy Spirit,
enflame my heart
and unite it to yourself!
I proclaim, eternal God,
that your power is powerful and strong enough
to free your Church and your people,
to snatch us from the devil's hand,
to stop the persecution of holy Church,
and to give me strength and victory
over my own enemies.
I proclaim that the wisdom of your son,
who is one with you,
can enlighten the eye of my understanding
and that of your people,
and can relieve the darkness of your sweet bride.
And I proclaim, eternal gentle goodness of God,
that the clemency of the Holy Spirit,
your blazing charity,
wants to enflame my heart
and everyone's
and unite them with yourself.

Power of you, eternal Father;
wisdom of your only-begotten Son
in his precious blood;
clemency of the Holy Spirit,
fire and deep well of charity
that held this Son of yours
fixed and nailed to the cross—
you know how to
and you can
and you want to,
so I plead with you:
have mercy on the world
and restore the warmth of charity
and peace
and unity
to holy Church.
O me!
I wish you would not delay any longer!
I beg you,
let your infinite goodness force you
not to close the eye of your mercy!

Gentle Jesus!
Jesus love!

                                                        (P 5)

O Holy Spirit, Come Into My Heart

O Holy Spirit, come into my heart;[6]
by your power draw it to yourself, God,
and give me charity with fear.

---

6. This short Trinitarian prayer is said to have been written by Catherine
   herself while all the other prayers were written down by others who
   listened as she prayed aloud. At the time of writing it she was at Rocca di
   Tentennano, south of Siena, on a difficult mission of reconciliation.

Guard me, Christ, from every evil thought,
and so warm and enflame me again
with your most gentle love
that every suffering may seem light to me.
My holy Father and my gentle Lord,
help me in my every need.
Christ love! Christ love!

(P 6)

Purify Your Vicar

O eternal love,
purify this vicar of yours[7]
in himself
so that he may give the others a good example
of purity and innocence.
May he serve willingly in your presence.
May he instruct the people subject to him,
and even attract unbelievers with heavenly teachings,
and offer to your unfathomable majesty
the fruit of [their] eternal salvation.

(P 7)

You Want to Renew the Church

O Godhead!
Godhead!
Eternal godhead!
True love!

7. The pope, Christ's vicar, for whom Catherine is praying here is Urban VI who succeeded Gregory XI.

Through the union of the humanity of your Word,
our Lord Jesus Christ,
with your all-powerful Godhead,
you have given to us who were lost
the light of most holy faith,
the pupil of the eye of our understanding,
with which we see and know our soul's true goal,
your immeasurable Godhead.
And you have made this Son of yours
a spotless sacrifice for us,
establishing him as the cornerstone
and firmest pillar of stability
for holy mother Church,
your one bride.
Long ago you decided to renew this Church
with new and more fruitful plants,
and from that time on
no one could break your most holy will,
eternal and unchangeable. . . .[8]

You are a fire always burning.
Yet,
though you always consume
all that the soul possesses apart from you,
you never consume
the things that are pleasing to you.
Burn with the fire of your Spirit
and consume,
root out from the bottom up,
every fleshly love and affection
from the hearts of the new plants
you have kindly seen fit
to set into the mystic body of holy Church.
Transplant them
away from worldly affections

---

8. Catherine prayed this passionate prayer for the renewal of the Church
   while she was in Rome soon after the beginning of the schism. The plants
   she refers to are most probably the cardinals created by the valid pope,
   Urban VI, in September 1378.

into the garden of your own affection,
and give them a new heart
with true knowledge of your will.
Make them despise the world
and themselves
and selfish love.
Fill them with your love's true fervor
and make them zealous for faith and virtue.
And so,
once they have left behind
the false desires and pretenses
of this passing world,
let them follow you alone
in purest purity
and glowing charity. . . .

So that you may deign to listen to these things,
supreme goodness,
true God,
I, poor as I am,
give you thanks for all of them.
Amen.

(P 7)

You Are Direct Without Any Twisting

O immeasurable love!
O gentle love!
Eternal fire!
You are that fire ever blazing,
O high eternal Trinity!
You are direct
without any twisting,
genuine
without any duplicity,
open

without any pretense.[9]
Turn the eye of your mercy on your creatures.
I know that mercy is your hallmark,
and no matter where I turn
I find nothing but your mercy.
This is why I run crying to your mercy
to have mercy on the world.[10]

You want us to serve you
in your way,
eternal Father,
and you guide your servants in different ways
along different paths.
And so today you show us
that we neither may nor can in any way judge
what is within a person
by the actions we see (cf. Rom 14:10; Is 11:3).[11]
Rather we should judge all things according to your will—
and most of all where your servants are concerned
who are united with your will
and transformed in it.
This is why the soul is happy
when in your light she sees the light
of the endlessly different ways and paths
she sees in these servants of yours.

For though they travel by different ways,
they are all running along the fiery road
of your charity;
otherwise they would not be following your truth
in truth. . . .
O eternal Truth,

---

9. In this prayer, Catherine celebrates both God's truth and God's mercy, two divine attributes which are very dear to her.
10. Catherine sees God as a God of infinite mercy longing to show mercy to the world.
11. A dominant Catherinian teaching is that we have no right or duty to judge others' motivation. In the *Dialogue* God tells her "Compassion is what you must have, you and the others, and leave the judging to me" (D 105).

what is your teaching
and what is the way
by which you want us to go to the Father,
the way by which we must go?
I know of no other road
but the one you paved
with the true and solid virtues
of your charity's fire.
You, eternal Word,
cemented it with your blood,
so this must be the road.
Our sin lies in nothing else
but in loving what you hate
and hating what you love.
I confess, eternal God,
that I have constantly loved what you hate
and hated what you love.
But today I cry out in the presence of your mercy:
grant that I may follow your truth
with a simple heart;
give me the deep well and fire of charity;
give me a continual hunger
to endure pains and torments for you.
Eternal Father,
give my eyes a fountain of tears
with which to draw your mercy down
over all the world.

(P 9)

How Fitting Mercy Is to You!

O eternal Godhead,
how fitting mercy is to you![12]

---

12. This prayer and chapter 30 of the *Dialogue* are considered to be among the finest tributes to God's mercy to be found in spiritual literature.

It suits you so well
that your servants arouse your mercy
against the judgment the world deserves
because of its sins!
Your mercy rules over us
and holds back your justice,
keeping the earth from opening up to swallow us,
keeping the animals from devouring us.
In fact, all things serve us
and the earth gives us its fruits.
All this your mercy does.
Your mercy preserves us
and prolongs our life.
giving us time to return and be reconciled with you.

O compassionate merciful Father,
who keeps the angels from taking revenge
on this humanity which is your enemy?
Your mercy.
In mercy you grant us consolation to coax us to love,
for the creature's heart
is attracted by love.
The same mercy gives and permits sufferings and hardships
so that we may learn to know ourselves
and acquire the little virtue of true humility—
and even to give yourself a reason
to reward those who fight bravely,
suffering with true patience.
In mercy you preserved the scars in your Son's body
so that he might with these scars
beg for mercy for us before your majesty (cf. Heb 7:25).
In mercy you have seen fit today to show me,
poor as I am,
how we can in no way pass judgment
on other people's intentions.
Indeed, by sending people along an endless variety of paths,
you give me an example for myself,
and for this I thank you.
Your mercy did not will

that the spotless Lamb should redeem the human race
with just a single drop of his blood,
nor with pain in just one part of his body,
but with his whole body's pain and blood.
Thus he would make complete atonement
for the whole human race
that had sinned against you.
We see that some of your creatures sin against you
with their hands,
others with their feet,
others with their head,
others with other parts of their body—
so the human race had sinned against you
with every part of the body.
Besides,
since every sin is committed with the will,
without which there would be no sin,
and since this will embraces the whole body,
therefore the whole human body sins against you.
This is why you wanted to make atonement
with the whole of your Son's body and blood;
thus everything would be fully atoned for
by the power of the infinite divine nature
joined with finite human nature.
In the Word
our humanity endured the pain
and the Godhead accepted the sacrifice. . . .

I have sinned against the Lord.
Have mercy on me!
Do not look at our sins,
all-powerful, compassionate, merciful God!
Amen.

(P 9)

In Your Light I See Light

Eternal Godhead!
O high eternal Godhead!
Boundless love!
In your light I have seen light;
in your light I have come to know the light (cf. Ps 36:10).[13]
In your light
we come to know the source of light
and the source of darkness—
that you are the source of all light,
and we the source of darkness.
In your light
we come to know what light does in the soul,
and what darkness does (cf. Jn 3:19-21, 115).
Your works are wonderful, eternal Trinity!
In your light they are known
because they come forth from you who are light.

Today your Truth, with wonderful light,
points out the source of darkness,
that stinking garment,
the selfish will.
And your Truth reveals as well
the means by which we come to know the light,
the garment of your gentle will.
What a marvelous thing,
that even while we are in the dark
we should know the light!
that in finite things
we should know the infinite!
that even while we exist in death
we should know life!
Your Truth shows us
that the soul must strip herself of her selfish will
if she wants to be clothed perfectly in yours,

---

13. This whole prayer eulogizes God's light.

just as one turns one's garment inside out
when one undresses (cf. Eph 4:22-24).
And how do we so strip ourselves?
By the light which we receive
when with the hand of free choice
we use the light we received in holy baptism—
for in the light we have seen light.
And from what source does the soul receive this light?
Only from you who are light—
and you have revealed this light to us
under the veil of our own humanity.
And what does the soul receive
who has been clothed in this light?
She is relieved of darkness
and hunger
and thirst
and death.
For hunger for virtue
drives out hunger for her selfish will;
thirst for your honor
drives out thirst for her own honor;
and the life of your grace
has driven out the death of sin
and of her own disordered will. . . .

O God eternal,
in your light I have seen
how closely you have conformed your creature
to yourself.
I see that you have set us, as it were,
in a circle,
so that wherever we may go
we are still within this circle.[14]
If I set myself to know in your light
the being you have given us,

14. In the *Dialogue* Catherine explains that the circle in which we exist is the
circle of self-knowledge in God: "You can go round and round this circle,
finding neither end nor beginning, yet never leaving the circle" (D 10).

I see that you have granted us the gift
of fashioning us after your own image and likeness,
sharing yourself,
eternal Trinity,
in the soul's three powers (Gn 1:26; cf. D 13).
If I consider the Word,
through whom we are created anew to grace,
I see you fashioned after us
and us after you
through the union that you, eternal God,
have effected with humankind.
And if I turn to the soul
enlightened by you, true light,
I see her making her continual dwelling place in you
by following your Truth's teaching,
generally as well as particularly—
I mean in particular virtues,
proved by the love
that the soul has conceived in your light.
And you are love itself.
So the soul who follows your Truth's teaching
in love
becomes through love
another you.
Dispossessed of her own will,
she is so well clothed in yours
that she neither seeks nor desires anything
but what you seek and will for her. . . .

Thanks,
thanks to you,
high eternal Trinity,
for in your light you have refreshed my soul
by letting me see how we,
your creatures,
are conformed with you,
and by teaching me how surpassing wonderful is your will.
I am the one who is not,

and you are the one who is.[15]
Do you yourself then
offer yourself thanks
by giving me the ability to praise you. . . .
I have sinned against the Lord.
Have mercy on me!
High eternal Godhead,
grant us your gentle benediction.
Amen.

(P 11)

My Nature Is Fire

In your nature,
eternal Godhead,
I shall come to know my nature
And what is my nature, boundless love?
It is fire,
because you are nothing but a fire of love.[16]
And you have given humankind
a share in this nature,
for by the fire of love
you created us.
And so with all other people
and every created thing;
you made them out of love.
O ungrateful people!
What nature has your God given you?
His very own nature!

---

15. This concept of God as the one who is and the human person as the one who is not is the basis of all Catherine's teaching on self-knowledge. Cf. Raymond of Capua, *Life* I, X, 92.

16. The image of fire is dear to Catherine. God is a fire of love who gives light, warmth, healing (cf. D 167). Being created in God's image, we too have natures of fire. We are true to our nature when we love.

Are you not ashamed
to cut yourselves off from such a noble thing
through the guilt of deadly sin?
O eternal Trinity,
my sweet love!
You, light,
give us light.
You, wisdom,
give us wisdom.
You, supreme strength,
strengthen us.
Today, eternal God,
let our cloud be dissipated
so that we may perfectly know and follow your Truth
in truth,
with a free and simple heart.

God, come to our assistance!
Lord, make haste to help us!
Amen.

(P 12)

Your Greatness Is Everywhere

O fire ever blazing!
The soul who comes to know herself in you
finds your greatness wherever she turns,
even in the tiniest things,
in people
and in all created things,
for in all of them she sees
your power
and wisdom
and clemency.
For if you had not been powerful,
knowing,

and willing,
you would not have created them.
But you were powerful and knowing and willing,
and therefore you created everything.[17]
O my poor blind soul,
you have never come to know yourself in him
because you have not stripped yourself
of your disordered will,
and have not clothed yourself
in his will. . . .

Eternal goodness,
you want me to gaze into you
and see that you love me,
to see that you love me gratuitously,
so that I may love everyone
with the very same love.[18]
You want me, then,
to love and serve my neighbors gratuitously,
by helping them
spiritually and materially
as much as I can,
without any expectation of selfish profit or pleasure.
Nor do you want me to hold back
because of their ingratitude or persecution,
or for any abuse I may suffer from them.
What then shall I do
to come to such a vision?
I shall strip myself
of my stinking garment,
and by the light of most holy faith
I shall contemplate myself in you.
And I shall clothe myself in your eternal will,

---

17. In this section on the Trinity, as in many other places, Catherine attributes
    power to the Father who can do all things, wisdom to the Son who knows
    all things, and clemency to the Holy Spirit who compassionately wills all
    that is good.
18. Catherine reflects here, in God's presence, on the depth and extent of love
    that we owe our neighbor.

and by this light I shall come to know
that you, eternal Trinity,
are table
and food
and waiter for us.[19]
You, eternal Father,
are the table
that offers us as food
the Lamb, your only-begotten Son.
He is the most exquisite of foods for us,
both in his teaching,
which nourishes us in your will,
and in the sacrament
that we receive in holy communion,
which feeds and strengthens us
while we are pilgrim travelers in this life.
And the Holy Spirit
is indeed a waiter for us,
for he serves us this teaching
by enlightening our mind's eye with it
and inspiring us to follow it.
And he serves us charity for our neighbors
and hunger to have as our food
souls
and the salvation of the whole world
for the Father's honor.
So we see that souls enlightened in you,
true light,
never let a moment pass
without eating this exquisite food
for your honor.

                                        (P 12)

---

19. Here we find another triple image for the Trinity: the Father is the table
    which offers us food, the Son is the food both in his teaching and in the
    eucharist, the Holy Spirit is the waiter who serves us the food (cf. D 78).

You Saw Me in Yourself

You, eternal God,
saw me and knew me
in yourself.
And because you saw me in your light
you fell in love with your creature
and drew her out of yourself
and created her in your image and likeness.[20]
But this did not make it possible
for me your creature
to know you in myself
except as I saw in myself
your image and likeness.
The lowliness of my understanding
could neither behold nor comprehend
your exaltedness.
Therefore,
so that I might see and know you in myself
and thus have perfect knowledge of you,
you made yourself one with us
by descending from your Godhead's great exaltedness
to the very lowliness of our humanity's clay.
So that I, then,
with my littleness,
would be able to see your greatness,
you made yourself a little one,
wrapping up the greatness of your Godhead
in the littleness of our humanity.[21]
Thus were you revealed to us
in the Word,
your only-begotten Son.
Thus have I come to know you,

20. Here, as elsewhere, Catherine gives her own very beautiful
    understanding of creation.
21. Catherine sees the incarnation as the essential means by which we come
    to know God.

deep well of charity,
within myself,
in this Word.

(P 13)

Our Wills Are Strong
When They Dwell in Yours

I acknowledge, eternal God;
I acknowledge, eternal God, high eternal Trinity,
that you see me and know me.
I have seen this in your light. . . .
I see too
that you saw that perverse law in us
that is always ready to rebel against your will,
and you saw
that we would often follow that law (cf. Rom 7:22-23).
Truly I see
that you saw the weakness of this human nature of ours,
how weak and frail and poor it is.
This is why,
supreme provider
who have provided for your creature in everything,
and best of helpers
who have given us help for every need—
this is why you gave us
the strong citadel of our will
as a partner for this weakness of our flesh.
For our will is so strong
that neither the devil nor any other creature
can conquer it
unless we so choose—
unless free choice,
in whose hand this strength has been put,
consents to it.[22]

---

22. Catherine attaches great importance to the fact that in our wills we have

O infinite goodness!
Where is the source of such strength
in your creature's will?
In you,
supreme and eternal strength!
So I see
that our will shares in the strength of yours,
for out of your will
you gave us ours.
So we see that our will is strong
to the extent that it follows yours,
and it is weak
to the extent that it departs from yours.
For, as I have said,
out of your own will you created ours,
and therefore ours is strong
when it dwells in yours.
All these things I have seen
in your light.
In our will,
eternal Father,
you reveal the strength of your will.
For if you have given such strength
to a tiny member,
how great should we reckon your own to be—
you who are Creator and ruler of all things!

One thing I see in your light:
this will, which you have given us as free,
seems to receive its strength
from the light of faith,
for by this light
we come in your light to know your eternal will,
and we see that your will wants nothing else
but that we be made holy (cf. 1 Thes 4:3).[23]
So the light strengthens the will

_____

freedom of choice. No one can take that freedom away from us (cf. D 14, 43, 144; L 69, 122).
23. "This is the will of God, your salvation."

and makes it grow,
and the will,
nourished by the light of holy faith,
gives life to our human actions.
So there can be neither a true will
nor a living faith
without action.
This light of faith
nourishes the fire within the soul
and makes it grow,
for we cannot feel the fire of your charity
unless the light shows us
your love and affection for us.

                                                    (P 14)

Make My Heart Big, Not Stingy

You, light, make the heart simple,
not two-faced.
You make it big,
not stingy—
so big that it has room in its loving charity
for everyone:
with well-ordered charity
it seeks everyone's salvation,
and because light is never without prudence
and wisdom,
it is ready to give its body up to death
for the salvation of a neighbor's soul,
but will not give its soul up to sin—
for we are not allowed to commit the least sin
even to save the whole world
(if that were possible),
since it is not right to offend the Creator,
who is all good,

for the benefit of creatures,
who are nothing by themselves.
But for a neighbor's physical good,
such a heart will give up its material possessions.
Such a heart is so open
that it is false to no one;
everyone can understand it
because it never says something different
with its face or tongue
from what it has within.
It shows that it has truly been stripped
of its old garment
and is clothed in the new garment
of your will.
So our cruelty, eternal Father,
springs from our failure to see
the compassion you have shown our souls
by buying them back
with your only-begotten Son's precious blood.

(P 15)

O Mary, Bearer of the Fire

O Mary!
Mary!
Temple of the Trinity!
O Mary, bearer of the fire!
Mary, minister of mercy!
Mary, seedbed of the fruit! . . .[24]

O Mary, peaceful sea!
Mary, giver of peace!
Mary, fertile soil!

---

24. Catherine prayed this prayer on the feast of the Annunciation the year
    before she died.

You, Mary, are the new-sprung plant
from whom we have the fragrant blossom,
the Word, God's only-begotten Son,
for in you, fertile soil,
was this Word sown.
You are the soil
and you are the plant.
O Mary, chariot of fire,
you bore the fire
hidden and veiled
under the ashes of your humanness.

O Mary, vessel of humility!
In you the light of true knowledge
thrives and burns.
By this light
you rose above yourself,
and so you were pleasing to the eternal Father,
and he seized you and drew you to himself,
loving you with a special love.
With this light
and with the fire of your charity
and with the oil of your humility
you drew his divinity
to stoop to come into you—
though even before that
he was drawn by the blazing fire
of his own boundless charity
to come to us.

O Mary,
because you had this light
you were prudent,
not foolish.[25]
Your prudence made you want to find out
from the angel

---

25. Cf. Mt 25:1-13 which tells the parable of the five prudent and the five
   foolish virgins.

how what he had announced to you
could be possible.
Didn't you know
that the all-powerful God could do this?
Of course you did,
without any doubt!
Then why did you say,
"since I do not know man"?
Not because you were lacking in faith,
but because of your deep humility,
and your sense of your own unworthiness.
No,
it was not because you doubted that God could do this.
Mary,
was it fear that troubled you
at the angel's word?
If I ponder the matter in the light,
it doesn't seem it was fear
that troubled you,
even though you showed some gesture of wonder
and some agitation.
What, then, were you wondering at?
At God's great goodness,
which you saw.
And you were stupefied
when you looked at yourself
and knew how unworthy you were
of such great grace.[26]
So you were overtaken
by wonder and surprise
at the consideration of your own unworthiness
and weakness
and of God's unutterable grace.

26. In this passage Catherine develops one of her favorite themes, self-knowledge. Just as we, in our cell of self-knowledge, come to know our greatness and our smallness, so at the moment of the incarnation does Mary know both her unworthiness and her dignity.

So by your prudent questioning
you showed your deep humility.
And, as I have said,
it was not fear you felt
but wonder at God's boundless goodness and charity
toward the lowliness and smallness
of your virtue.

You, O Mary,
have been made a book
in which our rule is written today.[27]
In you today
is written the eternal Father's wisdom;
in you today
our human strength and freedom are revealed.
I say that our human dignity is revealed
because if I look at you, Mary,
I see that the Holy Spirit's hand
has written the Trinity in you
by forming within you
the incarnate Word, God's only-begotten Son.
He has written for us the Father's wisdom,
which this Word is;
he has written power for us,
because he was powerful enough
to accomplish this great mystery;
and he has written for us
his own—the Holy Spirit's—clemency
for by divine grace and mercy alone
was such a great mystery
ordained and accomplished. . . .

In you, O Mary,
our human strength and freedom
are today revealed,
for after the deliberation

_____

27. Jesus Christ is the "rule" written in Mary's book.

of such and so great a council,
the angel was sent to you
to announce to you
the mystery of the divine counsel
and to seek to know your will,
and God's Son
did not come down into your womb
until you had given your will's consent.
He waited at the door of your will
for you to open to him;
for he wanted to come into you,
but he would never have entered unless you had opened to him,
saying,
"Here I am,
God's servant;
let it be done to me
as you have said" (Lk 1:38). . . .

O Mary,
may you be proclaimed blessed among all women
for endless ages,
for today you have shared with us
your flour.
Today the Godhead
is joined and kneaded into one dough
with our humanity—
so securely
that this union could never be broken,
either by death
or by our thanklessness.
In fact,
the Godhead was united
even with Christ's body in the tomb
and with his soul in limbo,
and afterward
with both his soul and body.
The relationship was so entered into
and sealed

that it will never be dissolved,
any more than it has been broken up to now.
Amen.

(P 18)

You Have Shown Us Love in Your Blood

You have shown us love
in your blood,
and in your blood
you have shown us your mercy
and generosity.[28]
In this blood
you have shown how our sin weighs you down.
In this blood
you have washed the face of your spouse, the soul,
with whom you are joined
by the union of the divine nature
with our human nature.
In this blood you clothed her
when she was naked,
and by your death
you restored her to life. . . .

O Passion!
You relieve every weakness,
if only the sick one wants to be healed—
for your gift
has not deprived us of liberty!
Yet more:
you, Passion, restore life

---

28. Catherine prayed this prayer on Passion Sunday (the second Sunday
    before Easter), the year before she died. In it her deep appreciation of
    Christ's redemptive death and its consequences for humankind comes
    through clearly.

to the dead.
If the soul becomes ill
because of the devil's temptations,
you deliver her.
If she is being hounded by the world
or besieged by her own weakness,
you are a refuge for her.
For the soul has come to know in you
not only what the Word did in his Passion—
which was finite—
but she has experienced besides
the height of divine charity.
So because of you, Passion,
she wants to know and understand the truth,
to be drunk on and dissolved in God's charity. . . .
Get up![29]
Get up out of the darkness!
Rouse yourself;
open the eye of your understanding
and look into the depth
within the deep well of divine charity.
For unless you see,
you cannot love.
The more you see,
the more you will love.
Once you love,
you will follow,
and you will clothe yourself in his will.

I have sinned, Lord.
Have mercy on me!
Amen.

(P 19)

---

29. Here Catherine, overwhelmed by God's love in Christ's passion,
    addresses herself.

To You, Eternal Father, I Offer My Life

O God eternal,
O good master!
You made and shaped the vessel of your creature's body
from the clay of the earth.
O tenderest love!
Of such a lowly thing you shaped it,
and then you put within it
no less a treasure than the soul,
the soul that bears the image of you,
God eternal.
You, good master,
my sweet love—
you are the master who breaks and refashions;
you smash this vessel
and put it back together again
as it pleases your goodness.

To you, eternal Father,
I offer once again my life,[30]
poor as I am,
for your dear bride.
As often as it pleases your goodness,
drag me out of this body
and send me back again,
each time with greater suffering than before,
if only I may see the reform
of this dear bride, holy Church.
I beg you, God eternal:
give me this bride.

---

30. Catherine made this self-offering to God for the sake of the Church during
the time of the schism. In it we see how she identifies her own broken
body with the brokenness of disunity in the Church. She also prays
tenderly and compassionately for her friends and followers. She died
about three months after saying this prayer.

Then, too,
I commend to you my children,
whom I love so much.
I pray you, most high eternal Father,
if it does please your mercy and goodness
to take me out of this vessel
and not make me go back again,
do not leave them orphans.
Visit them with your grace
and make them live as if they were dead,
in true and most perfect light.
Bind them together
with the gentle chain of charity,
so that they may have eager courage to die
within this dear bride.
I beg you, eternal Father,
let none of them be snatched from my hands.

Forgive us all our sins,
and forgive me the great foolishness and neglect
of which I have been guilty in your Church—
for I have not done
what I could and should have done.
I have sinned against the Lord.
Have mercy on me!

I offer and commend to you my children,
whom I so love,
for they are my soul.
But should it please your goodness
to make me stay yet longer in this vessel,
then do you, best of doctors,
heal and care for it,
for it is all shattered.
Give,
O give to us, eternal Father,
your gentle benediction.
Amen.

(P 26)

The Dialogue

The Dialogue is Catherine of Siena's principal work. It can be regarded as a compendium of all her theological teaching. It is called *The Dialogue* because its contents are in the form of a dialogue between Catherine (who refers to herself in the third person) and God. In it she addresses God most often as "father," and she is addressed as "daughter." Throughout the book, one notices a close familiarity between the two: in one place (chapter 30), she tells God that she feels free to babble on and on because she is sure of being listened to with immense love and mercy. There is even a deeper reason why this work is fittingly called *The Dialogue*, namely, it tells of the great dialogue initiated by God with humanity in which Jesus Christ is the reconciling, peace-making Word.

Contrary to a pious legend that *The Dialogue* was composed during a five-day ecstasy, historical evidence indicates that it was probably dictated by Catherine over a period of many months between December 1377 and October 1378. There is a definite structure to this book. In its introduction she sets the stage by making four petitions to God: for herself, for the Church, for the whole world, and for the assurance of God's providence in all things, with particular regard for a certain person whose need she is aware of. The rest of the book is taken up with God's response to these four petitions, with, every now and then, an interjection from Catherine. At the end there is a short conclusion which brings the principal themes together. Within this broad structure, as G. Cavallini (see below) has conclusively shown, there is a recurring pattern of petition-response-thanksgiving.[1]

Although Catherine's style of writing is colorful, fresh and vigorous, *The Dialogue* can make for difficult reading. In some places, it is wordy and repetitious; in others, it has an abundance of long, complicated sentences. Sometimes too, conclusions seem to be reached without the necessary preparatory steps, so that it is not always easy

---

1. G. Cavallini, *Il Dialogo*, xiv. See also S. Noffke, *Catherine of Siena—The Dialogue*, 15.

to follow Catherine's line of thought. For these reasons, *The Dialogue* is a book to be dipped into and prayed with, rather than to be read from cover to cover. It is hoped that the passages which appear on the following pages will help the reader to appreciate some of the nuggets of theological and spiritual gold buried in *The Dialogue*.

In 1968 a critical edition of *The Dialogue* in Italian was edited by Giuliana Cavallini: *Il Dialogo*. The Introduction to this edition is invaluable in its explanation of the structure and contents of Catherine of Siena's great work. This critical edition had been translated into English and edited by Suzanne Noffke: *Catherine of Siena—The Dialogue*. It is from this translation that the following passages have been taken. The location of each passage is indicated by D followed by the relevant chapter-number.

Overwhelming Love

You said, "Let us make humankind in our image and likeness" (Gn 1:26). And this you did, eternal Trinity, willing that we should share all that you are, high eternal Trinity! You, eternal Father, gave us memory to hold your gifts and share your power. You gave us understanding so that, seeing your goodness, we might share the wisdom of your only-begotten Son. And you gave us free will to love what our understanding sees and knows of your truth, and so share the clemency of your Holy Spirit.[2]

Why did you so dignify us? With unimaginable love you looked upon your creatures within your very self, and you fell in love with us. So it was love that made you create us and give us being just so that we might taste your supreme eternal good.[3]

Then I see how by our sin we lost the dignity you had given us. Rebels that we were, we declared war on your mercy and became your enemies. But stirred by the same fire that made you create us, you decided to give this warring human race a way to reconciliation, bringing great peace out of our war. So you gave us your only-begotten Son, your Word, to be mediator between us and you. He became our justice taking on himself the punishment for our injustices. He offered you the obedience you required of him in clothing him with our humanity, eternal Father, taking on our likeness and our human nature!

O depth of love! What heart could keep from breaking at the sight of your greatness descending to the lowliness of our humanity? We are your image, and now by making yourself one with us you have become our image, veiling your eternal divinity in the wretched cloud and dung heap of Adam. And why? For love! You, God, became human and we have been made divine! In the name of this unspeak-

---

2. As has already been noted, Catherine sees human persons in the threefold image of God. Through their memory they are in the image of the Father who is power; through their understanding they are in the image of the Son who is wisdom; through their will they are in the image of the Holy Spirit who is clemency and love.

3. Catherine regards love as the only motive for our creation.

able love, then, I beg you—I would force you even!—to have mercy on your creatures.

(D 13)

Where did she come to know this honor of being fused into the blood of the Lamb as she was baptized in the power of that blood? In his open side, where she came to know the fire of divine charity. This is what my Truth showed you, if you recall, when you asked him, "Why, gentle spotless Lamb, since you were dead when your side was opened, did you want your heart to be pierced and parted?"[4]

He answered, "There were plenty of reasons, but I shall tell you one of the chief. My longing for humankind was infinite, but the actual deed of bearing pain and torment was finite and could never show all the love I had. This is why I wanted you to see my inmost heart, so that you would see that I loved you more than finite suffering could show. . . .

"I showed you this in the opening up of my side. There you find my heart's secret and it shows you, more than any finite suffering could, how I love you. And I show you this without limit."

(D 75)

O eternal Father! O fiery abyss of charity! O eternal beauty, O eternal wisdom, O eternal goodness, O eternal mercy! O hope and refuge of sinners! O immeasurable generosity! O eternal, infinite Good! O mad lover! And you have need of your creature? It seems so to me, for you act as if you could not live without her, in spite of the fact that you are Life itself, and everything has life from you and nothing can have life without you. Why then are you so mad? Because you have fallen in love with what you have made! You are pleased and delighted over her within yourself, as if you were drunk [with desire] for her salvation.[5] She runs away from you and you go looking for her. She strays and you draw closer to her. You clothed yourself in our humanity, and nearer than that you could not have come.

---

4. Here Catherine is reflecting on Jn 19:34. She sees the piercing of Jesus' side as the way in which the love of his heart was manifested.

5. Catherine's anthropomorphic language is passionate and unrestrained: God is "mad" with love for us and "drunk" with desire for our salvation.

And what shall I say? I will stutter, "A-a," because there is nothing else I know how to say. Finite language cannot express the emotion of the soul who longs for you infinitely.

(D 153)

Unspeakable Mercy

Know that no one can escape my hands, for I am who I am, whereas you have no being at all of yourselves.[6] What being you have is my doing; I am the Creator of everything that has any share in being. But sin is not of my making, for sin is nonbeing. Sin is unworthy of any love, then, because it has no part in me. Therefore, my creatures offend me when they love sin, which they should not love, and hate me, to whom they owe love because I am supremely good and gave them being with such burning love. But they cannot escape me: Either I will have them in justice because of their sin, or I will have them in mercy.

Open the eye of your understanding, then, and look at my hand, and you will see that what I have told you is true.

So in obedience to the most high Father, she raised her eyes, and she saw within his closed fist the entire world. And God said:

My daughter, see now and know that no one can be taken away from me. Everyone is here as I said, either in justice or in mercy. They are mine; I created them, and I love them ineffably. And so, in spite of their wickedness, I will be merciful to them because of my servants, and I will grant what you have asked of me with such love and sorrow.

(D 18)

---

6. This is a fundamental teaching of Catherine. It connects with an experience she had in prayer in which Jesus Christ appeared to her and said, "Do you know, daughter, who you are and who I am? . . . You are the one who is not, and I am the one who is" (cf. Raymond of Capua, *Life* I, X, 92). This theme of self-knowledge in God runs through all her writings.

Then that soul stood before God as if intoxicated and, unable to restrain herself, she said:

O eternal Mercy, you who cover over your creatures' faults! It does not surprise me that you say of those who leave deadly sin behind and return to you: "I will not remember that you had ever offended me." O unspeakable mercy! I am not surprised that you speak so to those who forsake sin, when you say of those who persecute you: "I want you to pray to me for them so that I can be merciful to them." What mercy comes forth from your Godhead, eternal Father, to rule the whole world with your power!

By your mercy we were created. And by your mercy we were created anew in your Son's blood. It is your mercy that preserves us. Your mercy made your Son play death against life and life against death on the wood of the cross. In him life confounded the death that is our sin, even while that same death of sin robbed the spotless Lamb of his bodily life. But who was conquered? Death! And how? By your mercy!

Your mercy is life-giving. It is the light in which both the upright and sinners discover your goodness. Your mercy shines forth in your saints in the height of heaven. And if I turn to the earth, your mercy is everywhere. Even in the darkness of hell your mercy shines, for you do not punish the damned as much as they deserve.

You temper your justice with mercy. In mercy you cleansed us in the blood; in mercy you kept company with your creatures. O mad lover! It was not enough for you to take on our humanity: You had to die as well! Nor was death enough: You descended to the depths to summon our holy ancestors and fulfill your truth and mercy in them. Your goodness promises good to those who serve you in truth, so you went to call these servants of yours from their suffering to reward them for their labors!

I see your mercy pressing you to give us even more when you leave yourself with us as food to strengthen our weakness, so that we forgetful fools should be forever reminded of your goodness. Every day you give us this food, showing us yourself in the sacrament of the altar within the mystic body of holy Church. And what has done this? Your mercy.

O mercy! My heart is engulfed with the thought of you! For wherever I turn my thoughts I find nothing but mercy! O eternal Father, forgive my foolish presumption in babbling on so before you—but your merciful love is my excuse in the presence of your kindness.[7]

(D 30)

After thus expanding her heart a bit in singing the praises of God's mercy, the soul humbly waited for him to keep his promise. And in reply to her God said:

Dearest daughter, you have been carrying on about my mercy because I let you experience it when I said to you, "I beg you to pray to me on behalf of these people." But know that my mercy toward you is incomparably more than you can see, because your sight is imperfect and limited, and my mercy is perfect and without limit. So there can be no comparison except that of the finite to the infinite.

(D 31)

If you ask me whether one should abandon vocal prayer, since it seems not everyone is drawn to mental prayer, the answer is no. A person has to walk step by step. I know well that, because the soul is imperfect before she is perfect, her prayer is imperfect as well. She should certainly, while she is still imperfect, stay with vocal prayer so as not to fall into laziness, but she should not omit mental prayer. In other words, while she says the words she should make an effort to concentrate on my love, pondering at the same time her own sins and the blood of my only-begotten Son. There she will find the expansiveness of my charity and forgiveness for her sins. Thus self-knowledge and the consideration of her sins ought to bring her to know my goodness to her and make her continue her exercise in true humility.

Now I do not want her to think about her sins individually, lest her mind be contaminated by the memory of specific ugly sins. I mean that I do not want her to, nor should she, think about her sins either in general or specifically without calling to mind the blood and the

---

7. This hymn to God's mercy is a panegyric, unique in spiritual literature, in which Catherine eulogizes the inexhaustibility and delicacy of divine mercy (cf. P 9).

greatness of my mercy. Otherwise she will only be confounded. For if self-knowledge and the thought of sin are not seasoned with remembrance of the blood and hope for mercy, the result is bound to be confusion. And along with this comes the devil, who under the guise of contrition and hatred for sin and sorrow for her guilt leads her to eternal damnation. Because of this—though not this alone—she would end in despair if she did not reach out for the arm of my mercy.

This is one of the subtle deceptions the devil works on my servants. So for your own good, to escape his deceit and to be pleasing to me, you must keep expanding your heart and your affection in the immeasurable greatness of my mercy, with true humility. For know this: The devil's pride cannot tolerate a humble mind, nor can his confounding withstand the greatness of my goodness and mercy when a soul is truly hopeful.

(D 66)

The injustice [sinners] practiced during their lifetime so accuses their conscience that they dare not ask for anything but justice. I tell you, their shame and confusion is so great that their only hope is to put their trust in my mercy if only this one time in their whole life. Granted, because of their sins, it is really presumptuous, for those who have used the arm of mercy to offend can hardly call this putting their trust in mercy. It is more presumption than trust, but at least they have accepted mercy's action. Thus, if when they come to the point of death they acknowledge their sin and unload their conscience in holy confession, the offensiveness of their presumptuousness is removed and what remains is mercy. With this mercy they gain access to hope if only they are willing. If this were not the case there is no one who would not despair, and despair would bring eternal damnation with the devils.

Thus does my mercy work to bring them to hope during their lifetime. I do not do this to give them leave to abuse my mercy but so that charity and the consideration of my goodness may make them open up. But these wretches abuse my mercy to the full, for they use the hope my mercy has given them to sin against me. Still I keep them in hope of my mercy so that at the point of death they will have something to take hold of and will not be completely crushed by their reproach and so end in despair. For this sin of ultimate despair is much more displeasing to me and harmful to them than all the other evils they have committed. And this is why: Other sins are committed with some selfish sensual pleasure, and sometimes they are regretted, and they can be regretted in such a way that the regret will win my mercy. But the motive for despair is not weakness, because there is to be found in it no pleasure but only intolerable pain. Despair spurns my mercy by considering one's sinfulness greater than my goodness and mercy.

(D 132)

Gentle Providence

O my dearest daughter, as I have told you so often, I want to be merciful to the world and provide for my reasoning creatures' every need. But the foolish take for death what I give for life, and are thus cruel to themselves. I always provide, and I want you to know that what I have given humankind is supreme providence.[8] It was with providence that I created you, and when I contemplated my creature in myself I fell in love with the beauty of my creation. It pleased me to create you in my image and likeness with great providence. I provided you with the gift of memory so that you might hold fast my benefits and be made a sharer in my own, the eternal Father's power. I gave you understanding so that in the wisdom of my only-begotten Son you might comprehend and know what I the eternal Father want, I who gave you graces with such burning love. I gave you a will to love, making you a sharer in the Holy Spirit's mercy, so that you might love what your understanding sees and knows.

---

8. Catherine's teaching on God's providence is rooted in a spiritual experience she had in which she heard God say to her, "Daughter, think of me; if you do, I will immediately think of you." Raymond of Capua who recounts this experience gives Catherine's own interpretation of God's words: "Do not be anxious about the well-being of your body and soul, for I who know and can do all things will think of it and look after it most carefully. Your task is to keep thinking of me (Raymond of Capua, *Life* I, X, 97).

All this my gentle providence did, only that you might be capable of understanding and enjoying me and rejoicing in my goodness by seeing me eternally. And as I have told you many times, I wanted to make it possible for you to reach this goal.

(D 135)

This is the gift of my providence, which has seen to your need for salvation in so many different ways from the beginning of the world until today, and will continue to do so right up to the end. I, the true and just doctor, give you whatever I see your weakness needs to make you perfectly healthy and to keep you healthy. My providence will never fail those who want to receive it. Whoever wants to experience my goodness in my providence has only to look at those who hope in me, who knock and call out not just with words but with love enlightened by most holy faith. I do not mean those who knock and shout only with empty words, calling out to me, "Lord! Lord!" I tell you, unless they make their requests of me with some other virtue, I will acknowledge them not with mercy but with justice (cf. Mt 7:21-23; 25:11-12; Lk 6:46). So I tell you, my providence will not fail those who truly hope in me, but it will fail those who hope not in me but in themselves.

(D 136)

So my providence has ordained and provided in all things with great wisdom. I have given because I am rich and I was and am able to give, and my wealth is infinite. Everything was made by me, and without me nothing can exist. Therefore, if it is beauty you want, I am beauty. If you want goodness, I am goodness, for I am supremely good. I am wisdom. I am kind; I am compassionate; I am the just and merciful God. I am generous, not miserly. I give to those who ask of me, open to those who knock in truth, and answer those who call out to me. I am not ungrateful but grateful and mindful to reward those who will toil for me, for the glory and praise of my name. I am joyful, and I keep the soul who clothes herself in my will in supreme joy. I am that supreme providence who never betrays my servants' hope in me in soul or body. . . .

How can people see me feeding and nurturing the worm within the dry wood, pasturing the brute beasts, nourishing the fish in the sea, all the animals on the earth and the birds in the air, commanding the sun to shine on the plants and the dew to fertilize the soul, and not believe that I nourish them as well, my creatures made in my image and likeness? As a matter of fact, all this is done by my goodness to serve them. No matter where they turn, spiritually and materially they will find nothing but my deep burning charity and the greatest, gentle, true, perfect providence. But they do not see it, because they have let go of the light and do not let themselves see. This is why they are scandalized and hold back in their charity for their neighbors.[9] Their thoughts are greedily on tomorrow, though my Truth forbade this when he said, "Do not be concerned about tomorrow; each day has enough worries of its own" (Mt 6:34). He was reproaching you for your infidelity and showing you my providence and the shortness of time when he said, "Do not be concerned about tomorrow." It is as if my Truth were saying, "Do not be concerned about what you cannot be sure of having; today is enough." And he taught you to ask first for the kingdom of heaven, that is, a good holy life, for I your heavenly Father know well enough that you need these lesser things. That is why I made the earth and commanded it to give you its fruits.

These wretches who in their lack of trust hold back their hearts and hands from charity for their neighbors have never read the teaching given by the Word my Truth, because they are not following in his footsteps. They become insupportable even to themselves. And from this trusting in themselves rather than in me comes every evil.

(D 141)

Trust in God

This is the sign that people's trust is in me rather than in themselves: that they have no slavish fear. Those who trust in themselves are afraid of their own shadow; they expect both heaven and earth to let them down. This fear and perverted trust in their scant wisdom makes them so wretchedly concerned about acquiring and holding

---

9. Here Catherine makes an essential connection between trust in God's providence and charity toward neighbor.

on to temporal things, that they seem to toss the spiritual behind their backs. Not one of them has any concern for the spiritual.

They forget, these faithless proud wretches, that I am the one who provides for everything that may be needed for soul or body. In the measure that you put your trust in me, in that measure will my providence be meted out to you. But these presumptuous wretches do not reflect that I am who I am and they are the ones who are not. From my goodness they have received their very being and every gift beyond that. So consider it useless to wear yourself out guarding your city unless it is guarded by me. Every effort is useless for those who think they can guard their city by their own toil or concern, for I alone am the guardian.

I have given you your being and other gifts beyond that, and it is true that I want you to use these by virtuously exercising my gift of free choice by the light of reason. For I created you without your help, but I will not save you without your help.[10] I loved you before you came into being. . . .

The only ones who are afraid are those who think they are alone, who trust in themselves and have no loving charity. They are afraid of every little thing because they are alone, deprived of me. For it is I who give complete security to the soul who possesses me in love. These my glorious loved ones experienced well that nothing could harm their souls. Indeed, they were the bane of humans and devils alike, who often were left chained by the strength and power I had given my servants over them. This was because I responded to the love and faith and trust they had put in me.

(D 119)

The Circle of Self-Knowledge

Imagine a circle traced on the ground, and in its center a tree sprouting with a shoot grafted into its side. The tree finds its nourish-

---

10. Cf. Augustine, Sermon 169, XI, 13, "The one who created you without your help will not save you without your help." This is a favorite maxim of Catherine.

ment in the soil within the expanse of the circle, but uprooted from
the soil it would die fruitless. So think of the soul as a tree made for
love and living only by love.[11] Indeed, without this divine love, which
is true and perfect charity, death would be her fruit instead of life. The
circle in which this tree's root, the soul's love, must grow is true
knowledge of herself, knowledge that is joined to me, who like the
circle have neither beginning nor end. You can go round and round
within this circle, finding neither end nor beginning, yet never leaving
the circle. This knowledge of yourself, and of me within yourself, is
grounded in the soil of true humility, which is as great as the expanse
of the circle (which is the knowledge of yourself united with me, as I
have said). But if your knowledge of yourself were isolated from me
there would be no full circle at all. Instead, there would be a beginning
in self-knowledge, but apart from me it would end in confusion.[12]

So the tree of charity is nurtured in humility and branches out in
true discernment. The marrow of the tree (that is, loving charity
within the soul) is patience, a sure sign that I am in her and that she
is united with me.

This tree, so delightfully planted, bears many-fragranced blossoms
of virtue. Its fruit is grace for the soul herself and blessing for her
neighbors in proportion to the conscientiousness of those who would
share my servants' fruits. To me this tree yields the fragrance of glory
and praise to my name, and so it does what I created it for and comes
at last to its goal, to me, everlasting Life, life that cannot be taken from
you against your will.

(D 10)

As the soul comes to know herself she also knows God better, for
she sees how good he has been to her. In the gentle mirror of God she
sees her own dignity: that through no merit of hers but by his creation
she is the image of God. And in the mirror of God's goodness she sees
as well her own unworthiness, the work of her own sin. For just as

---

11. Catherine sees self-knowledge in God as the only way to grow in love of
God and neighbor.
12. Self-knowledge and God-knowledge are complementary. The one cannot
exist without the other in the Christian life. As a person grows in love, the
two fuse more and more into one knowledge.

you can better see the blemish on your face when you look at yourself in a mirror, so that soul who in true self-knowledge rises up with desire to look at herself in the gentle mirror of God with the eye of understanding sees all the more clearly her own defects because of the purity she sees in him.

(D 13)

You ask for the will to know and love me, supreme Truth. Here is the way, if you would come to perfect knowledge and enjoyment of me, eternal Life: Never leave the knowledge of yourself. Then, put down as you are in the valley of humility you will know me in yourself, and from this knowledge you will draw all that you need.

(D 4)

You cannot arrive at virtue except through knowing yourself and knowing me. And this knowledge is more perfectly gained in time of temptation, because then you know that you are nothing, since you have no power to relieve yourself of the sufferings and troubles you would like to escape. And you know me in your will, when I strengthen it in my goodness so that it does not consent to these thoughts. You realize that my love has granted them, for the devil is weak and can do nothing of himself, but only as I permit him. And I give him leave not through hatred but through love, not so that you may be conquered but that you may conquer and come to perfect knowledge of yourself and of me, and to prove your virtue—for virtue can only be tested by its opposite.

(D 43)

The soul cannot live without love. She always wants to love something because love is the stuff she is made of, and through love I created her. This is why I said that it is affection that moves the understanding, saying, as it were, "I want to love, because the food I feed on is love." And the understanding, feeling itself awakened by affection, gets up, as it were, and says, "If you want to love, I will give you something good that you can love." And at once it is aroused by the consideration of the soul's dignity and the indignity into which she has fallen through her own fault. In the dignity of her existence she tastes the immeasurable goodness and uncreated love with which I created her. And in the sight of her own wretchedness she discovers and tastes my mercy, for in mercy I have lent her time and drawn her out of darkness.

(D 51)

You cannot imagine how great is people's foolishness. They have no sense or discernment, having lost it by hoping in themselves and putting their trust in their own knowledge. O stupid people, do you not see that you are not the source of your own knowledge? It is my goodness, providing for your needs, that has given it to you.

What shows you this? That which you experience in yourselves: Say you want to do something you neither can do nor know how to do. Sometimes you have the knowledge but not the ability, and at other times you have the ability but not the knowledge. Sometimes you do not have time, or if you have the time you lack the desire. I grant all this to provide for your salvation, so that you may know that you are nothing of yourselves and may have reason to humble yourselves and not become proud. So you find change and privation in everything, for things are not at your command. Only my grace is firm and stable and cannot be taken away from you or changed unless you change it by departing from this grace and turning to sin.

How, then, can you lift up your head against my goodness? You cannot, if you would follow reason, nor can you put your hope in yourselves or trust in your own knowledge. But because you have become senseless beasts you do not see that all things except my grace are changing. And why do you not put your trust in me your Creator? Because your trust is in yourselves. Am I not faithful and loyal to you? Of course I am. And this is not hidden from you because you experience it continually.

(D 140)

Sometimes my providence leaves my great servants a pricking, as I did to my gentle apostle Paul, my chosen vessel. After he had received my Truth's teaching in the depths of me the eternal Father, I still left him the pricking and resistance of his flesh (cf. 2 Cor 12:7).[13]

Could I and can I not make it otherwise for Paul and the others in whom I leave this or that sort of pricking? Yes. Then why does my providence do this? To give them opportunity for merit, to keep them in the self-knowledge whence they draw true humility, to make them compassionate instead of cruel toward their neighbors so that they will sympathize with them in their labors. For those who suffer themselves are far more compassionate to the suffering than are those who have not suffered. They grow to greater love and run to me all anointed with humility and ablaze in the furnace of my charity. And through these means and endless others they attain perfect union.

(D 145)

Christ the Bridge

I told you that I have made a bridge of the Word, my only-begotten Son, and such is the truth.[14] I want you to realize, my children, that by Adam's sinful disobedience the road was so broken up that no one could reach everlasting life. Since they had no share in the good for which I had created them, they did not give me the return of glory they owed me, and so my truth was not fulfilled. What is this truth? That I had created them in my image and likeness so that they might have eternal life, sharing in my being and enjoying my supreme eternal tenderness and goodness. But because of their sin they never reached this goal and never fulfilled my truth, for sin closed heaven and the door of my mercy.

This sin sprouted thorns and troublesome vexations. My creatures

---

13. In the passage that follows, in which she gives her own interpretation of Paul's thorn in the flesh (2 Cor 12:7), Catherine illustrates the necessary connection between knowledge of our weakness and compassion toward others.

14. Basing herself on Jn 14:6, "I am the way ... ," Catherine presents Jesus Christ as the bridge who unites in his person, and through his redemptive death, God and humanity. An understanding of her teaching on Christ as the bridge is necessary in order to appreciate her Christology.

found rebellion within themselves, for as soon as they rebelled against me, they became rebels against themselves. Their innocence lost, the flesh rebelled against the spirit and they became filthy beasts. All created things rebelled against them, whereas they would have been submissive if all had been kept as I had established it in the beginning. But they stepped outside my obedience and so deserved eternal death in both soul and body.

With sin there came at once the flood of a stormy river that beat against them constantly with its waves, bringing weariness and troubles from themselves as well as from the devil and the world. You were all drowning, because not one of you, for all your righteousness, could reach eternal life.

But I wanted to undo these great troubles of yours. So I gave you a bridge, my Son, so that you could cross over the river, the stormy sea of this darksome life, without being drowned.

See how indebted to me my creatures are! And how foolish to choose to drown rather than accept the remedy I have given!

(D 21)

I want you to look at the bridge of my only-begotten Son, and notice its greatness. Look! It stretches from heaven to earth, joining the earth of your humanity with the greatness of the Godhead. This is what I mean when I say it stretches from heaven to earth—through my union with humanity.

This was necessary if I wanted to remake the road that had been broken up, so that you might pass over the bitterness of the world and reach life. From earth alone I could not have made it great enough to cross the river and bring you to eternal life. The earth of human nature by itself, as I have told you, was incapable of atoning for sin and draining off the pus from Adam's sin, for that stinking pus had infected the whole human race. Your nature had to be joined with the height of mine, the eternal Godhead, before it could make atonement for all of humanity. Then human nature could endure the suffering, and the divine nature, joined with that humanity, would accept my Son's sacrifice on your behalf to release you from death and give you life.

So the height stooped to the earth of your humanity, bridging the chasm between us and rebuilding the road. And why should he have made of himself a roadway? So that you might in truth come to the same joy as the angels. But my Son's having made of himself a bridge for you could not bring you to life unless you make your way along that bridge.

(D 22)

And how was heaven opened? With the key of his blood. So, you see, the bridge has walls and a roof of mercy. And the hostelry of holy Church is there to serve the bread of life and the blood, lest the journeying pilgrims, my creatures, grow weary and faint on the way. So has my love ordained that the blood and body of my only-begotten Son, wholly God and wholly human, be administered.

I explained all this to you, you will recall, because I wanted to let you see the way. So when he says that he is the Way he is speaking the truth. And I have already shown you that he is the Way, in the image of a bridge. He says he is Truth, and so he is, and whoever follows him goes the way of truth. And he is Life (cf. Jn 14:6). If you follow this truth you will have the life of grace and never die of hunger, for the Word has himself become your food. Nor will you ever fall into darkness, for he is the light undimmed by any falsehood. Indeed, with his truth he confounds and destroys the lie with which the devil deceived Eve. That lie broke up the road to heaven, but Truth repaired it and walled it up with his blood.

Those who follow this way are children of the truth because they follow the truth. They pass through the gate of truth and find themselves in me. And I am one with the gate and the way that is my son, eternal Truth, a sea of peace.

But those who do not keep to this way travel below through the river—a way not of stones but of water. And since there is no restraining the water, no one can cross through it without drowning.

(D 27)

Now you have seen and heard what you asked of me, that is, how you should behave if you would not drown. I have told you that this is the way: to climb up onto the bridge. In this climbing up you are all gathered together and united, loving each other, carrying your hearts and wills like vessels to me (who give anyone to drink who asks), keeping to the way of Christ crucified with perseverance even till death.

This is the way you must all keep to no matter what your situation, for there is no situation that rules out either your ability or your obligation to do so. You can and you must, and every person gifted with reason has this obligation. No one can draw back saying, "My position or my children or other earthly obstacles keep me from following this way." Nor can the difficulties you encounter along this way excuse you. You are not to talk that way, because I have already told you that every state of life is pleasing and acceptable to me if it is held to with a good and holy will. For all things are good and perfect, since they were made by me, and I am supreme Goodness. I made them and gave them to you not for you to use them to embrace death, but that you might have life through them.

It is an easy matter, for nothing is as easy and delightful as love. And what I ask of you is nothing other than love and affection for me and for your neighbors. This can be done any time, any place, and in any state of life by loving and keeping all things for the praise and glory of my name.

(D 55)

You cannot see me as I am. This is why I covered the divine nature with the veil of your humanity, so that you would be able to see me. I who am invisible made myself, as it were, visible by giving you the Word, my Son, veiled in your humanity. He showed me to you. And this is why he did not say, "I will show you the Father," but, "I will show myself to you." It is as if he had said, "I will show myself to you in accordance with what the Father has given me" (Jn 14:8-9).

So you see, when he showed me, he showed himself.

(D 62)

Stages on the Journey

Now I want to tell you about those who have begun to climb the stairway and want to follow the perfect road by actually living out the counsels as well as the commandments. I will show you these in three stages, explaining to you specifically now the three degrees or stages of the soul[15] and the three stairs that I have already set before you more generally in terms of the soul's three powers. The first of these stages is imperfect, the second more perfect, and the third most perfect. The first is a mercenary, the second my faithful servant, and the third my child who loves me with no regard for selfish interests.

These are three stages for which many have the capacity, and all three can be present in one and the same person. This is done when a person runs along the way perfectly careful to make good use of time, and from the mercenary stage reaches the free, and from the free the filial.

Rise up above yourself. Open your mind's eye and watch how these pilgrims travel: some imperfectly, some perfectly in the way of the commandments, and some most perfectly by keeping and practicing the way of the counsels. You will see what is the source of imperfection and what the source of perfection. And you will see how deluded is the soul from whom the root of selfish love has not been dug up. No matter what your state in life, it is essential to kill this selfish love in yourself.

(D 56)

I told you that no one can cross over the bridge and so escape the river without climbing the three stairs. Such is the truth, and some climb imperfectly, some perfectly, and others with great perfection.

But there are many who begin their climb so sluggishly and pay what they owe me in such bits and pieces, so indifferently and ignorantly, that they quickly fall by the way. The smallest wind makes them hoist their sails and turn back. They had climbed only imper-

---

15. On the bridge of Christ crucified, Catherine sees three steps: the feet, the heart, the mouth. Those three steps are sometimes identified with the three classical stages in the spiritual life: purification, illumination, union.

fectly to the first stair of Christ crucified, and so they never reach the
second, which is that of his heart.

(D 59)

Now it remains to say how one can tell that a soul has attained
perfect love. The sign is the same as that given to the holy disciples
after they had received the Holy Spirit. They left the house and
fearlessly preached my message by proclaiming the teaching of the
Word, my only-begotten Son. They had no fear of suffering. No, they
even gloried in suffering. It did not worry them to go before the
tyrants of the world to proclaim the truth to them for the glory and
praise of my name.

So it is with the soul who has waited for me in self-knowledge: I
come back to her with the fire of my charity. In that charity she
conceived the virtues through perseverance when she stayed at home,
sharing in my power. And in that power and virtue she mastered and
conquered her selfish sensual passion.

In that same charity I shared with her the wisdom of my Son, and
in that wisdom she saw and came to know, with her mind's eye, my
truth and the delusions of spiritual sensuality, that is, the imperfect
love of one's own consolation. And she came to know the malice and
deceit the devil works on the soul who is bound up in that imperfect
love. So she rose up in contempt of that imperfection and in love for
perfection.

I gave her a share in this love, which is the Holy Spirit, within her
will by making her will strong to endure suffering and to leave her
house in my name to give birth to the virtues for her neighbors. Not
that she abandons the house of self-knowledge, but the virtues conceived by the impulse of love come forth from that house. She gives
birth to them as her neighbors need them, in many different ways. For
the fear she had of not showing herself lest she lose her own consolations is gone. After she has come to perfect, free love, she lets go of
herself and comes out, as I have described.

And this brings her to the fourth stage. That is, after the third stage,
the stage of perfection in which she both tastes and gives birth to
charity in the person of her neighbor, she is graced with a final stage
of perfect union with me. These two stages are linked together, for the

one is never found without the other any more than charity for me can exist without charity for one's neighbors or the latter without charity for me. The one cannot be separated from the other. Even so, neither of these two stages can exist without the other.

(D 74)

Three Kinds of Relationship: Servant, Friend, Child [16]

There are others who become faithful servants. They serve me with love rather than that slavish fear which serves only for fear of punishment. But their love is imperfect, for they serve me for their own profit or for the delight and pleasure they find in me. Do you know how they show that their love is imperfect? By the way they act when they are deprived of the comfort they find in me. And they love their neighbors with the same imperfect love. This is why their love is not strong enough to last. No, it becomes lax and often fails. It becomes lax toward me when sometimes, to exercise them in virtue and to lift them up out of their imperfection, I take back my spiritual comfort and let them experience struggles and vexations. I do this to bring them to perfect knowledge of themselves, so that they will know that of themselves they have neither existence nor any grace. I want them, in time of conflict, to take refuge in me by seeking me and knowing me as their benefactor, in true humility seeking me alone. This is why I give them these troubles. And though I may take away their comfort, I do not take away grace.

If these souls do not give up the exercise of holy prayer and other good works, but go on strengthening their virtue perseveringly, they will come to filial love. And I will love them as my children, because with whatever love I am loved, with that love I respond. If you love me the way a servant loves a master, I as your master will give you what you have earned, but I will not show myself to you, for secrets are shared only with a friend who has become one with oneself.

Still, servants can grow because of their virtue and the love they

16. While the three steps may symbolize the three stages of the spiritual life, in Catherine's theology they can be better seen as indicating three possible relationships with God.

bear their master, even to becoming his very dear friend. So it is with
these souls. As long as their love remains mercenary I do not show
myself to them. But they can, with contempt for their imperfection
and with love of virtue, use hatred to dig out the root of their spiritual
selfishness. They can sit in judgment on themselves so that motives
of slavish fear and mercenary love do not cross their hearts without
being corrected in the light of most holy faith. If they act in this way,
it will please me so much that for this they will come to the love of
friendship.

And then I will show myself to them, just as my Truth said: "Those
who love me will be one with me and I with them, and I will show
myself to them and we will make our dwelling place together." This
is how it is with very dear friends. Their loving affection makes them
two bodies with one soul, because love transforms one into what one
loves. And if these souls are made one soul [with me], nothing can be
kept hidden from them. This is why my Truth said, "I will come and
we will make a dwelling place together." That is the truth.

(D 60)

Now you have seen what a superb state they are in who have
attained the love of friendship. They have mounted the feet of their
affection and climbed as far as the secret of his heart, the second of
the three stairs. I have told you the meaning of the soul's three powers,
and now I would suggest to you that the stairs symbolize the three
stages through which the soul advances.

But before I go on to the third stair I want to show you how a person
comes to be my friend, and once my friend, becomes my child by
attaining filial love. I want to show you what makes a person my
friend and how you will know that you have become my friend.

First I will tell you how a soul comes to be my friend. In the
beginning she was imperfect, living in slavish fear. By dint of practice
and perseverance she came to the love of pleasure and self-advantage,
because in me she found both pleasure and profit. This is the path
those must travel who wish to attain perfect love, the love of friendship and filial love.

Filial love, I tell you, is perfect. For with filial love one receives the
inheritance from me the eternal Father. But no one attains filial love

without the love of friendship, and this is why I told you that one progresses from being my friend to becoming my child.

(D 63)

When a soul has reached the third stage, the love of friendship and filial love, her love is no longer mercenary. Rather she does as very close friends do when one receives a gift from the other. The receiver does not look just at the gift, but at the heart and the love of the giver, and accepts and treasures the gift only because of the friend's affectionate love. So the soul, when she has reached the third stage of perfect love, when she receives my gifts and graces does not look only at the gift but with her mind's eye looks at the affectionate charity of me, the Giver.

And so that you might have no excuse for not looking at my affection, I found a way to unite gift and giver: I joined the divine nature with the human. I gave you the Word, my only-begotten Son, who is one with me and I with him, and because of this union you cannot look at my gift without looking at me, the Giver.

See, then, with what affectionate love you ought to love and desire both the gift and the giver! If you do, your love will be pure and genuine and not mercenary. This is how it is with those who keep themselves always shut up in the house of self-knowledge.

(D 72)

Now this is how the soul acts who has in truth reached the third stair. This is the sign that she has reached it: Her selfish will died when she tasted my loving charity, and this is why she found her spiritual peace and quiet in the mouth. You know that peace is given with the mouth. So in this third stage the soul finds such a peace that there is nothing that can disturb her. She has let go of and drowned her own will, and when that will is dead there is peace and quiet.

She brings forth virtue for her neighbors without pain. Not that this is in itself painless, but the dead will feels no pain because it endures pain willingly for my name's sake.

She runs briskly along the way of the teaching of Christ crucified.

Nor does she slacken her pace for any assault that may befall her, or any persecution, or any pleasure the world may offer her. All these things she overcomes with true strength and patience, her will clothed in my loving charity and enjoying the food of the salvation of souls in true and perfect patience. Such patience is a sure sign that the soul loves me perfectly and without self-interest, for if she loved me and her neighbors for her own profit she would be impatient and would slacken her pace.

But she loves me for myself, because I am supreme Goodness and deserve to be loved, and she loves herself and her neighbors because of me, to offer glory and praise to my name. And therefore she is patient and strong in suffering, and persevering.

(D 76)

At the first step they put off love of vice from the feet of their affection. At the second they taste the secret and the love of his heart and there conceive love in virtue. At the third step of spiritual peace and calm they prove their virtue, and rising up from imperfect love they come to great perfection. Thus have these found rest in the teaching of my Truth. They have found table and food and waiter,[17] and they taste this food through the teaching of Christ crucified, my only-begotten Son.

I am their bed[18] and table. This gentle loving Word is their food, because they taste the food of souls in this glorious Word and because he himself is the food I have given you: his flesh and blood, wholly God and wholly human, which you receive in the sacrament of the altar, established and given to you by my kindness while you are pilgrims and travelers, so that you may not slacken your pace because of weakness, nor forget the blessing of the blood poured forth for you with such

---

17. This trinitarian image of the Father as the table, the Son as the food, and the Holy Spirit as the waiter is used by Catherine to bring out important qualities attributed to each of the three persons of the Trinity. This imagery points to the "availability" of the Trinity to us.

18. Here Catherine describes the Father as our "bed." In one of her letters (L 73) she speaks of the Holy Spirit as our "bed." In both cases she is indicating that God is the one in whom we can rest and who will support us no matter how heavy or burdened we feel.

burning love, but may be constantly strengthened and filled with pleasure as you walk. The Holy Spirit, my loving charity, is the waiter who serves them my gifts and graces.

This gentle waiter carries to me their tender loving desires, and carries back to them the reward for their labors, the sweetness of my charity for their enjoyment and nourishment. So you see, I am their table, my Son is their food, and the Holy Spirit who proceeds from me the Father and from the Son, waits on them.

(D 78)

Sin and its Consequences

I would have you know that every virtue of yours and every vice is put into action by means of your neighbors. If you hate me, you harm your neighbors and yourself as well (for you are your chief neighbor), and the harm is both general and particular.[19]

Sin is both in the mind and in the act. You have already sinned in your mind when you have conceived a liking for sin and hatred for virtue. (This is the fruit of that sensual selfishness which has driven out the loving charity you ought to have for me and your neighbors.) And once you have conceived you give birth to one sin after another against your neighbors, however it pleases your perverse sensual will. Sometimes we see cruelty, general or particular, born. It is a general sort of cruelty to see yourself and others damned and in danger of death for having lost grace. What cruelty, to refuse to help either oneself or others by loving virtue and hating vice! But some actually extend their cruelty even further, not only refusing the good example of virtue but in their wickedness assuming the role of the devil by dragging others as much as they can from virtue and leading them to vice. This is spiritual cruelty: to make oneself the instrument for depriving others of life and dealing out death.

Bodily cruelty springs from greed, which not only refuses to share

---

19. Catherine explains the three-fold consequence of sin: God is offended, one's neighbor is harmed and one deprives oneself of grace.

what is one's own but takes what belongs to others, robbing the poor, playing the overlord, cheating, defrauding, putting up one's neighbors' goods—and often their very persons—for ransom.

O wretched cruelty! You will find yourself deprived of my mercy unless you turn to compassion and kindness! At times you give birth to hurtful words, followed often enough by murder. At other times you give birth to indecency toward others, and the sinner becomes a stinking beast, poisoning not only one or two but anyone who might approach in love or fellowship.

And who is hurt by the offspring of pride? Only your neighbors. For you harm them when your exalted opinion of yourself leads you to consider yourself superior and therefore to despise them. And if pride is in a position of authority, it gives birth to injustice and cruelty, and becomes a dealer in human flesh.

O dearest daughter, grieve that I am so offended, and weep over these dead so that your prayer may destroy their death! For you see that everywhere, on every level of society, all are giving birth to sin on their neighbors' heads. For there is no sin that does not touch others, whether secretly by refusing them what is due them, or openly by giving birth to the vices of which I have told you.

It is indeed true, then, that every sin committed against me is done by means of your neighbors.

(D 6)

A Call to Repentance

And what causes sinners to be so unfortunate and blind that they do not know this treasure? The cloud of selfish love and wretched pride that made them depart from obedience and fall into disobedience. Because they are not obedient they are not patient, and in their impatience they suffer intolerably. It has drawn them away from the way of truth and leads them along the way of falsehood so that they become servants and friends of the devils, and unless they change their ways, in their disobedience they will go along with their masters the devils to eternal punishment. But my beloved children who are obedient to the Law rejoice and exult in the eternal sight of me with the humble spotless Lamb, the maker, fulfiller, and giver of the Law. In this life they have tasted peace in its observance, and in the blessed life they receive and are clothed in the most perfect peace. Here there is peace without any war, every good without any evil, security without any fear, wealth without poverty, satiety without boredom, hunger without pain, light without darkness, supreme Good not finite but infinite, shared by all the truly joyful.

What has established them in such a great reward? The blood of the Lamb by whose power the key of obedience shed its rust so that you would be able to use it to unlock the gate. So it is obedience that has opened it for you by the power of the blood.

O stupid fools! Do not wait any longer to come up out of the filthy mire. It seems you roll about in the mire of sensuality as pigs roll about in the mud. Leave behind injustice and murders, hatred and spite, the detraction, complaining, [rash] judgment, and violence you have used against your neighbors, the thievery and betrayal and perverse pleasures and delights of the world. Cut off pride's horns and so dissipate the hatred you have in your hearts for those who do you harm. Compare the harm you do to me and to your neighbors with what is done to you, and you will find that in comparison to what you do to me and them your own hurt is nothing. It is easy to see that by harboring hatred you insult me because you violate my commandment, and you hurt your neighbors by depriving them of loving charity. I commanded you to love me above all things and to love your neighbors as your very selves. This was not qualified in any way that might say: If they hurt you, do not love them. No, [your love must be] free and sincere, because the command was given you by my Truth, who observed it with sincerity. You ought to observe it with the same sincerity, for if you do not, you are hurting yourselves and harming your souls by depriving yourselves of the life of grace.

(D 156)

Jesus' Obedience and Ours

When I saw that humankind, whom I so loved, was not returning to me its end, my infinite goodness constrained me to put the key of obedience into the hand of the gentle loving Word, my Truth, and he like a doorman unlocked heaven's gate. Without this key and this doorman, my Truth, no one can enter. This is why he said in the holy gospel that no one can come to me, the Father, except through him. When he rose beyond human companionship through his ascension to return triumphantly to me into heaven, he left you this sweet key of obedience. . . .

In him, then, you will find this virtue in her fullness. He left her to you as a rule and teaching that he first lived himself. She is a straight path leading to life. And he is himself the Way. This is why he said that he is Way and Truth and Life and that whoever walks by this way walks in the light (Jn 14:6). Those who walk in the light cannot unwittingly stumble or be tripped up, because they have cast off the darkness of selfish love that had been the cause of their falling into disobedience. For, as I have told you, the source and companion of obedience is humility. But disobedience comes from pride, which in turn comes from selfish love for oneself and deprives one of humility. Selfish love gives disobedience impatience as a sister and pride as wet nurse. And in the darkness of infidelity she runs along the darksome way that leads to eternal death.

All of you ought to read this glorious book [the Word], for here you will find this and all the other virtues written.

(D 154)

Charity Gives Life to All the Virtues

No virtue can have life in it except from charity, and charity is nursed and mothered by humility. You will find humility in the knowledge of yourself when you see that even your own existence comes not from yourself but from me, for I loved you before you came into being. And in my unspeakable love for you I willed to create you anew in grace. So I washed you and made you a new creation in the blood that my only-begotten Son poured out with such burning love.

This blood gives you knowledge of the truth when knowledge of yourself leads you to shed the cloud of selfish love. There is no other way to know the truth. In so knowing me the soul catches fire with unspeakable love, which in turn brings continual pain. Indeed, because she has known my truth as well as her own sin and her neighbors' ingratitude and blindness, the soul suffers intolerably. Still, this is not a pain that troubles or shrivels up the soul. On the contrary, it makes her grow fat. For she suffers because she loves me, nor would she suffer if she did not love me.

(D 4)

I have told you how every sin is done by means of your neighbors, because it deprives them of your loving charity, and it is charity that gives life to all virtue. So that selfish love which deprives your neighbors of your charity and affection is the principle and foundation of all evil.

Every scandal, hatred, cruelty, and everything unbecoming springs from this root of selfish love. It has poisoned the whole world and sickened the mystic body of holy Church and the universal body of Christianity. For all virtues are built on charity for your neighbors. So I have told you, and such is the truth: Charity gives life to all the virtues, nor can any virtue exist without charity. In other words, virtue is attained only through love of me. . . .

Virtue, once conceived, must come to birth. Therefore, as soon as the soul has conceived through loving affection, she gives birth for her neighbors' sake. And just as she loves me in truth, so also she serves her neighbors in truth. Nor could she do otherwise, for love of me and love of neighbor are one and the same thing: Since love of neighbor has its source in me, the more the soul loves me, the more she loves her neighbors.

(D 7)

Love of Neighbor

It is your duty to love your neighbors as your own self. In love you ought to help them spiritually with prayer and counsel, and assist them spiritually and materially in their need—at least with your good will if you have nothing else. If you do not love me you do not love your neighbors (cf. 1 Jn 2:9-11; 4:20-21),[20] nor will you help those you do not love. But it is yourself you harm most, because you deprive yourself of grace. And you harm your neighbors by depriving them of the prayer and loving desires you should be offering to me on their behalf. Every help you give them ought to come from the affection you bear them for love of me.

In the same way, every evil is done by means of your neighbors, for you cannot love them if you do not love me. This lack of charity for me and for your neighbors is the source of all evils, for if you are not doing good you are necessarily doing evil. And to whom is this evil shown and done? First of all to yourself and then to your neighbors—not to me, for you cannot harm me except insofar as I count whatever you do to them as done to me. You do yourself the harm of sin itself, depriving yourself of grace, and there is nothing worse you can do. You harm your neighbors by not giving them the pleasure of the love and charity you owe them, the love with which you ought to be helping them by offering me your prayer and holy desire on their behalf. Such is the general help that you ought to give to every reasoning creature.

More particular are the services done to those nearest you, under your very eyes. Here you owe each other help in word and teaching and good example, indeed in every need of which you are aware, giving counsel as sincerely as you would to yourself, without selfishness. If you do not do this because you have no love for your neighbors, you do them special harm, and this as persistently as you refuse them the good you could do.

(D 6)

---

20. In the history of spirituality Catherine of Siena stands out as one who is particularly insistent on the truth that love of God and love of neighbor are intrinsically connected. They are the two feet that we need to walk through this life in a way that pleases God.

Drink Your Neighbor's Love in God

I would have you know that every [good], whether perfect or imperfect, is acquired and made manifest in me. And it is acquired and made manifest by means of your neighbor. Even simple folk know this, for they often love others with a spiritual love. If you have received my love sincerely without self-interest, you will drink your neighbor's love sincerely. It is just like a vessel that you fill at the fountain. If you take it out of the fountain to drink, the vessel is soon empty. But if you hold your vessel in the fountain while you drink, it will not get empty: indeed, it will always be full. So the love of your neighbor, whether spiritual or temporal, is meant to be drunk in me, without any self-interest.[21]

I ask you to love me with the same love with which I love you. But for me you cannot do this, for I loved you without being loved. Whatever love you have for me you owe me, so you love me not gratuitously but out of duty, while I love you not out of duty but gratuitously. So you cannot give me the kind of love I ask of you. This is why I have put you among your neighbors: so that you can do for them what you cannot do for me—that is, love them without any concern for thanks and without looking for any profit for yourself. And whatever you do for them I will consider done for me (cf. Mt 25:40).

My Truth demonstrated this when Paul was persecuting me and he said, "Saul, Saul, why are you persecuting me" (Acts 9:4)? For he considered Paul's persecution of my faithful ones as persecution of me.

So your love should be sincere: You should love your neighbors with the same love with which you love me. Do you know how you can tell when your spiritual love is not perfect? If you are distressed when it seems that those you love are not returning your love or not loving you as much as you think you love them. Or if you are distressed when it seems to you that you are being deprived of their company or comfort, or that they love someone else more than you.

From these and from many other things you should be able to tell if your love for me and for your neighbors is still imperfect and that

---

21. Catherine makes the point that we do not alternate love of God and love of neighbor, but rather that it is in God's love that we find love of others.

you have been drinking from your vessel outside of the fountain, even though your love was drawn from me. But it is because your love for me is imperfect that you show it so imperfectly to those you love with a spiritual love.

All this comes of the failure to dig out every bit of the root of spiritual selfishness. This is why I often permit you to form such a love, so that you may come through it to know yourself and your imperfection in the way I have described.

(D 64)

Our Interdependence is God's Will

Virtue, once conceived, must come to birth. Therefore, as soon as the soul has conceived through loving affection, she gives birth for her neighbors' sake. And just as she loves me in truth, so also she serves her neighbors in truth. Nor could she do otherwise, for love of me and love of neighbor are one and the same thing: Since love of neighbor has its source in me, the more the soul loves me, the more she loves her neighbors.

The same is true of many of my gifts and graces, virtue and other spiritual gifts, and those things necessary for the body and human life. I have distributed them all in such a way that no one has all of them. Thus have I given you reason—necessity, in fact—to practice mutual charity. For I could well have supplied each of you with all your needs, both spiritual and material. But I wanted to make you dependent on one another so that each of you would be my minister, dispensing the graces and gifts you have received from me. So whether you will it or not, you cannot escape the exercise of charity! Yet, unless you do it for love of me, it is worth nothing to you in the realm of grace.

So you see, I have made you my ministers, setting you in different positions and in different ranks to exercise the virtue of charity. For there are many rooms in my house (cf. Jn 14:2). All I want is love. In loving me you will realize love for your neighbors, and if you love your neighbors you have kept the law (cf. Mt 22:37-40). If you are bound by this love you will do everything you can to be of service wherever you are.

(D 7)

Keep in mind that each of you has your own vineyard. But every one is joined to your neighbors' vineyards without any dividing lines. They are so joined together, in fact, that you cannot do good or evil for yourself without doing the same for your neighbors.

All of you together make up one common vineyard, the whole Christian assembly, and you are all united in the vineyard of the mystic body of holy Church from which you draw your life. In this vineyard is planted the vine, which is my only-begotten Son, into whom you must be engrafted (cf. Rom 11:17-24). Unless you are engrafted into him you are rebels against holy Church, like members that are cut off from the body and rot.

(D 24)

Do Not Judge

The devil would like to catch you with this inviting hook, often making you pass judgment on something that is not there in your neighbors, and so you would scandalize them.

So let silence or a holy argument for virtue be in your mouth to discourage vice. And when you think you discern vice in others, put it on your own back as well as theirs, acting always with true humility.

I want you to know also that you should not trust everything you see. Rather put it behind your back and choose not to see it, holding fast only the sight and knowledge of yourself and my generosity and goodness to you. This is how those souls behave who have reached the final stage of which I have told you. Because they return continually to the valley of self-knowledge, their exaltation and union with me is never blocked.

(D 102)

I will, then, and so should you—you and my other servants—that you concentrate on coming to know yourselves perfectly, so that you may more perfectly know my goodness to you. Leave this and every other kind of judgment to me, because it is my prerogative, not yours (cf. Mt 7:1; Lk 6:41-42; Rom 12:19).[22] Give up judgment, which belongs to me, and take up compassion with hunger for my honor and the salvation of souls. And with restless longing preach virtue and reprove vice in yourself and in others in the manner I have just described for you.

(D 103)

I also told you, and I will tell you again, that nothing in the world can make it right for you to sit in judgment on the intentions of my servants, either generally or in particular, whether you find them well or ill disposed.

And I told you the reason you cannot judge, and that if you do you will be deluded in your judgment. But compassion is what you must have, you and the others, and leave the judging to me.

(D 105)

True Friendship

Whenever the soul loves someone with a special love, she feels pain when the pleasure or comfort or companionship she has become accustomed to, and which gave her great consolation, is lessened. Or she suffers if she sees that person keeping more company with someone else than with her. This pain makes her enter into knowledge of herself. And if she is willing to walk wisely in the light as she ought, she will come to love that special person more perfectly, for with self-knowledge and the contempt she has conceived for her selfish

---

22. For Catherine judgment of others' intentions and motives is never right. Such judgment stands in opposition to compassion. The *Dialogue*, cc. 98-108 deals extensively with the matter of judging others.

feelings, she will cast off imperfection and come to perfection. Once she is more perfect, a greater and more perfect love for others in general will follow, as well as for the special person my goodness has given her.

(D 144)

Members of One Body

I have shown you my generosity, goodness, and providence toward people. But they let themselves be guided by their own darksome weakness. Your bodily members put you to shame, because they all together practice charity, while you do not (cf. 1 Cor 12:14-26). Thus, when the head is aching, the hand helps it. And if the finger, that tiniest of members, hurts, the head does not snub it because it is greater and more noble than all the other parts of the body. No, it comes to its aid with hearing and sight and speech and everything it has. And so with all the other members. But those who are proud do not behave that way. They see a poor person, one of their members, sick and in need, and do not help. They refuse to give not only of their possessions but even a single word. Indeed, they reproachfully and scornfully turn away. They have plenty of wealth, but they leave the poor to starve. They do not see that their wretched cruelty throws filth into my face, and that their filth reaches down even to the depths of hell.

(D 148)

Fear of Losing One's Peace and Quiet

[Some] people find all their pleasure in seeking their own spiritual consolation—so much so that often they see their neighbors in spiritual or temporal need and refuse to help them. Under pretense of virtue they say, "It would make me lose my spiritual peace and quiet, and I would not be able to say my Hours at the proper time." Then if they do not enjoy consolation they think they have offended me. But they are deceived by their own spiritual pleasure, and they offend me more by not coming to the help of their neighbors' need than if they had abandoned all their consolations. For I have ordained every exercise of vocal and mental prayer to bring souls to perfect love for me and their neighbors, and to keep them in this love.

So they offend me more by abandoning charity for their neighbor for a particular exercise or for spiritual quiet than if they had abandoned the exercise for their neighbor. For in charity for their neighbors they find me, but in their own pleasure, where they are seeking me, they will be deprived of me. Why? Because by not helping they are by that very fact diminishing their charity for their neighbors. When their charity for their neighbors is diminished, so is my love for them. And when my love is diminished, so is consolation. So, those who want to gain lose, and those who are willing to lose gain. In other words, those who are willing to lose their own consolation for their neighbors' welfare receive and gain me and their neighbors, if they help and serve them lovingly. And so they enjoy the graciousness of my charity at all times.

(D 69)

The Power of Intercession

I have one remedy to calm my wrath: my servants who care enough to press me with their tears and bind me with the chain of their desire.[23] You see, you have bound me with that chain—and I myself gave you that chain because I wanted to be merciful to the world. I put into my servants a hunger and longing for my honor and the salvation of souls so that I might be forced by their tears to soften the fury of my divine justice.

Bring, then, your tears and your sweat, you and my other servants. Draw them from the fountain of my divine love and use them to wash the face of my bride. I promise you that thus here beauty will be restored. Not by the sword or by war or by violence will she regain

---

23. In many places in her writings, Catherine teaches that God, who longs to show mercy to all, wants us to ask for that mercy for the Church and for the world.

her beauty, but through peace and through the constant and humble prayers and sweat and tears poured out by my servants with eager desire.

And so I will fulfill your desire by giving you much to suffer, and your patience will spread light into the darkness in all the world's evil.

(D 15)

I have satisfied your desire by responding to what you asked me, because I do not spurn my servants' desires. I give to those who ask, and even invite you to ask. And I am very displeased with those who do not knock in truth at the door of Wisdom, my only-begotten Son, by following his teaching. Following his teaching is a kind of knocking that calls out to me the eternal Father with the voice of holy desire in constant humble prayer. And I am that Father who gives the bread of grace through this door, my gentle Truth. Sometimes, to test your desires and your perseverance, I pretend not to hear you. But I do hear you, and I give you whatever you need, for it is I who gave you the very hunger and voice with which you call to me, and when I see your constancy I fulfill your desires insofar as they are ordered in accord with my will.

My Truth invited you to call out thus when he said, "Call and you will be answered; knock and it shall be opened to you; ask and it shall be given to you" (Mt 7:7-8; Lk 11:9-10). So I am telling you what I want you to do. Never relax your desire to ask for my help. Never lower your voice in crying out to me to be merciful to the world. Never stop knocking at the door of my Truth by following in his footsteps. Find your delight with him on the cross by feeding on souls for the glory and praise of my name. And with a restless heart bewail the death of this child, humanity, whom you see reduced to such misery that your tongue could not tell it.

Through this lamentation and crying out it is my will to be merciful to the world. This is what I require of my servants and this will be a sign to me that you love me in truth. Nor will I spurn your desires, as I have told you.

(D 107)

Now, I beg you, be merciful to the world and to holy Church. I am asking you to grant what you are making me ask. Alas for my wretched sorrowful soul, the cause of all evil! Do not delay any longer in granting your mercy to the world; bow down and fulfill the longing of your servants. Alas! It is you who make them cry out: so listen to their voices. Your Truth said that we should call and we would be answered, that we should knock and the door would be opened for us, that we should ask and it would be given to us. O eternal Father, your servants are calling to you for mercy. Answer them then, I know well that mercy is proper to you,[24] so you cannot resist giving it to whoever asks you for it. Your servants are knocking at the door of your Truth. They are knocking because in your Truth, your only-begotten Son, they have come to know your unspeakable love for humankind. Therefore your burning charity neither can nor should hold back from opening to those who knock with perseverance.

Open, then, unlock and shatter the hardened hearts of your creatures. If you will not do it for their failure to knock, do it because of your infinite goodness and for love of your servants who are knocking at your door for them. Grant it, eternal Father, because you see how they stand at the door of your Truth and ask (cf. Rv 3:20). And for what are they asking? For the blood of this door, your Truth.

(D 134)

I have already told you, if you recall, that it is by means of my servants and their great sufferings that I would be merciful to the world and reform my bride.

Truly these last can be called another Christ crucified, my only-begotten Son, because they have taken his task upon themselves. He came as a mediator to put an end to the war and reconcile humanity to me in peace by suffering even to the shameful death of crucifixion. In the same way must these be crucified and become mediators in prayer, in word, in good holy living.

(D 146)

---

24. In saying that mercy is proper to God, Catherine is making a profound theological statement, namely that God would not be God without the quality of mercy (cf. P 9).

The Qualities of Good Ministers in the Church

I told you that [my ministers] have taken on the qualities of the sun. Indeed, they are suns, for there is in them no darkness of sin or ignorance, because they follow the teaching of my Truth. Nor are they lukewarm, because they are set ablaze in the furnace of my charity. They have no use for the world's honors and ranks and pleasures. Therefore, they are not afraid to correct. Those who do not hanker after power or ecclesiastical rank have no fear of losing it. They reprove [sin] courageously, for those whose conscience does not accuse them of sin have nothing to fear.

So this pearl [of justice] was not clouded over in these anointed ones, these christs of mine, of whom I have told you.[25] No, it was luminous. They embraced voluntary poverty and sought after lowliness with deep humility. This is why they were not annoyed by people's derision or abuse or slander, or by insult or shame or pain or torture. They were cursed, and they blessed. They endured with true patience, like earthly angels and more than angels—not by nature, but because of the sacramental grace given them from above to be the stewards of the body and blood to my only-begotten Son.

How humbly they governed and communicated with their subjects! With what hope and lively faith! They had no fear or worry that either they or their subjects would be lacking in temporal goods, so they generously gave out the Church's possessions to the poor. Thus they fulfilled to the utmost their obligation to divide their temporal goods to meet their own needs and those of the poor and the Church. They set nothing aside, and after their death there was no great estate to settle; in fact, some of them left the Church in debt for the sake of the poor—all because of their generous charity and their trust in my providence. They were strangers to slavish fear, so they were confident they would lack nothing, either spiritually or temporally.

Because I had appointed them to such dignity for the salvation of souls, they never rested, good shepherds that they were, from gather-

---

25. Catherine is referring here to holy people of the past who showed themselves to be good ministers, and whose qualities are always needed in the Church.

ing the little sheep into the sheepfold of holy Church. In their love and hunger for souls they even laid down their lives to rescue them from the devils' hands (cf. Jn 10). They made themselves weak along with those who were weak. That is, to keep the weak from being confounded with despair and to give them more room to expose their weakness, they would show their own weakness, saying, "I am weak along with you." They wept with those who wept and rejoiced with those who rejoiced (cf. 1 Cor 9:22; Rom 12:15). Thus they knew how to give everyone the right food ever so tenderly. They encouraged the good by rejoicing in their goodness, for they were not gnawed up with envy but broad in the generosity of their charity for their neighbors and subjects. Those who were sinful they drew out of their sin by showing that they themselves were also sinful and weak. Their compassion was true and holy, and while correcting others and imposing penances for the sins they had committed, they themselves in their charity did penance along with them. Because of their love, they who were imposing the penance suffered more than those who received it. And sometimes some of them actually did the same penance themselves, especially when they saw that it seemed very difficult for the penitent. And by that act the difficulty became sweet for them.

(D 119)

Look at Dominic

And look at the ship of your father Dominic, my beloved son.[26] He governed it with a perfect rule, asking [his followers] to be attentive only to my honor and the salvation of souls with the light of learning. He wished to build his foundation on this light, while not for all that giving up true and voluntary poverty. He had that as well, and as a sign that he had it and that its opposite displeased him, he left as a bequest to his sons his curse and mine if they should have or keep any property individually or collectively. It was a token that he had chosen Queen Poverty as his bride.

---

26. Catherine was a lay Dominican, belonging to the Mantellate in Siena. She had a profound love of St. Dominic, and a deep appreciation of the Dominican vocation.

But for his more proper object he took the light of learning in order to stamp out the errors that were rising up at that time. He took up the task of the Word, my only-begotten Son. Clearly he appeared as an apostle in the world, with such truth and light did he sow my word, dispelling the darkness and giving light. He was a light that I offered the world through Mary and sent into the mystic body of holy Church as an uprooter of heresies. Why did I say "through Mary"? Because Mary gave him the habit—a task my goodness entrusted to her.

Where would he have his children eat by the light of learning? At the table of the cross. On that cross is set the table of holy desire where one eats souls for love of me. He wanted his children to do nothing else but stand at this table by the light of learning to seek only the glory and praise of my name and the salvation of souls. And so that they might attend to nothing else, he relieved them of worry about temporal things and wanted them to be poor. Was he lacking in faith or did he fear they would not be provided for? Certainly not, for he was clothed in faith and trusted firmly in my providence. . . .

So Dominic set his ship in order by rigging it with three strong ropes: obedience, continence, and true poverty. He made it thoroughly royal by not tying it to the guilt of deadly sin. Enlightened by me, the true light, he was providing for those who were less perfect. For, though all who observe the rule are perfect, still even in [this way of] life one is more perfect than another, and both the perfect and the not-so-perfect fare well on this ship. Dominic allied himself with my Truth by showing that he did not want the sinner to die but rather to be converted and live. He made his ship very spacious, gladsome, and fragrant, a most delightful garden. . . .

Consider the glorious Thomas.[27] With his mind's eye he contemplated my Truth ever so tenderly and there gained light beyond the natural and knowledge infused by grace. Thus he learned more through prayer than through human study. He was a blazing torch shedding light within his order and in the mystic body of holy Church, dispelling the darkness of heresies. . . .

I could tell you about many others who, though they never suffered actual martyrdom, did so in spirit, as did Dominic. What workers this

---

27. Thomas Aquinas, great Dominican theologian and saint, penetrated the depths of God's truth more through prayer than human study, as did Catherine herself.

father sent into his vineyard to uproot the thorns of vice and to plant
the virtues!

(D 158)

Benefits of the Eucharist

Dearest daughter, contemplate the marvelous state of the soul who
receives this bread of life, this food of angels, as she ought. When she
receives this sacrament she lives in me and I in her. Just as the fish is
in the sea and the sea in the fish, so am I in the soul and the soul in
me, the sea of peace.[28] Grace lives in such a soul because, having
received this bread of life in grace, she lives in grace. When this
appearance of bread has been consumed, I leave behind the imprint
of my grace, just as a seal that is pressed into warm wax leaves its
imprint when it is lifted off. Thus does the power of this sacrament
remain there in the soul; that is, the warmth of my divine charity, the
mercy of the Holy Spirit, remains there. The light of my only-begotten
Son's wisdom remains there, enlightening the mind's eye. [The soul]
is left strong, sharing in my strength and power, which make her
strong and powerful against her selfish sensuality and against the
devil and the world.

So you see, the imprint remains once the seal is lifted off. In other
words, once the material appearances of the bread have been consumed, this true Sun returns to his orbit. Not that he had ever left it,
for he is united with me. But my deep charity gave him to you as food
for your salvation and for your nourishment in this life where you are
pilgrim travelers, so that you would have refreshment and would not
forget the blessing of the blood. I in my divine providence gave you
this food, my gentle Truth, to help you in your need.

See, then, how bound and obligated you are to love me in return,
since I have loved you so much, and because I am supreme eternal
Goodness, deserving to be loved by you.

(D 112)

---

28. A similar idea is found in D 12.

Different Kinds of Tears[29]

First of all, there are the tears of damnation, the tears of this world's evil ones.

Second are the tears of fear, of those who weep for fear because they have risen up from the sin out of fear of punishment.

Third are those who have risen up from sin and are beginning to taste me. These weep tenderly and begin to serve me. But because their love is imperfect, so is their weeping.

The fourth stage is that of souls who have attained perfection in loving their neighbors and love me without any self-interest. These weep and their weeping is perfect.

The fifth stage (which is joined to the fourth) is that of sweet tears shed with great tenderness.

I will tell you, too, about tears of fire, shed without physical weeping, which often satisfy those who want to weep but cannot. And I want you to know that a soul can experience all of these different stages as she rises from fear and imperfect love to attain perfect love and the state of union.

(D 88)

Now you have seen the different kinds of tears and the differences among them, as it has pleased my truth to satisfy your desire.

The first kind of tears, the tears of those who are dead in sin, come from a heart that is corrupt. Now the heart is the source of all emotion, which in turn is the source of tears. So because these persons' heart is corrupt, the weeping that comes from it is corrupt and wretched, and so are all their actions.

The second kind of weeping is that of souls who are beginning to know their own sinfulness through the punishment that must be their lot after sinning. This is a common sort of beginning that I in my kindness grant to weak souls who like fools are drowning down there

29. In Catherine of Siena's teaching on tears, she distinguishes five different kinds of tears corresponding to five affective states of the soul. All but the first of these are salutary, and mark stages on a person's journey to God. Tears are for Catherine the most intense expression of the heart's feelings.

in the river because they shun my Truth's teaching. There are so very many who come as far as this sort of self-knowledge. Without slavish fear of their own punishment they would perish. Some, in a sudden great contempt for themselves, come to consider themselves deserving of punishment. There are others who give themselves in wholesome simplicity to serving me their Creator because they are sorry they have offended me. Those who go the way of great self-contempt are, it is true, more apt to reach perfection than the others. Both will reach it if they exert themselves, but the former will get there sooner. The first sort must take care not to rest in their slavish fear. The others must watch out for tepidity, for if they do not exercise their simplicity it will grow lukewarm within them. This is an ordinary sort of calling.

The third and fourth kinds of weeping belong to those who have risen above fear and attained to love and hope. They taste my divine mercy and receive from me many gifts and consolations, and because of these things their eyes, responding to the heart's emotion, weep. This weeping is still imperfect, because it is mixed with weeping that is spiritually sensual. But if these souls exercise themselves in virtue they reach the fourth stage, where, because their desire has grown, they so unite themselves with my will that they can no longer desire anything but what I will. They are clothed with a charity for their neighbors that gives birth in them to a lover's lament that I am offended and their neighbors hurt.

Such weeping is one with the fifth sort, that of ultimate perfection. Here the soul is united with Truth and the flame of holy desire burns more fiercely within her. The devil flees from this desire and can no longer persecute the soul—not by assaulting her, because love for her neighbors has made her patient, nor by using spiritual or temporal consolations, because she would spurn such things in contempt and true humility.

(D 90)

Desire Is Infinite

Do you not know, my daughter, that all the sufferings the soul bears or can bear in this life are not enough to punish one smallest sin? For an offense against me, infinite Good, demands infinite satisfaction. So I want you to know that not all sufferings given in this life are given for punishment, but rather for correction, to chastise the child who offends. However, it is true that a soul's desire, that is, true contrition and sorrow for sin, can make satisfaction. True contrition satisfies for sin and its penalty not by virtue of any finite suffering you may bear, but by virtue of your infinite desire. For God, who is infinite, would have infinite love and infinite sorrow.

The infinite sorrow God wills is twofold: for the offense you yourself have committed against your Creator, and for the offense you see on your neighbors' part. Because those who have such sorrow have infinite desire and are one with me in loving affection (which is why they grieve when they sin or see others sinning), every suffering they bear from any source at all, in spirit or in body, is of infinite worth, and so satisfies for the offense that deserved an infinite penalty. True, these are finite deeds in finite time. But because their virtue is practiced and their suffering borne with infinite desire and contrition and sorrow for sin, it has value.

(D 3)

I have told you about perfect and imperfect tears, and how they all come from the heart. Whatever their reason, they all come from this same vessel, and so all of them can be called "heartfelt tears." The only difference lies in whether the love is ordered well or ill, is perfect or imperfect.

I still have to tell you, if I would fully answer your desire, about some souls who want the perfection of tears though it seems they cannot have it. Is there another way than physical tears? Yes. There is a weeping of fire, of true holy longing, and it consumes in love. Such a soul would like to dissolve her very life in weeping in self-contempt and for the salvation of souls, but she seems unable to do it.

I tell you, these souls have tears of fire. In this fire the Holy Spirit weeps in my presence for them and for their neighbors. I mean that my divine charity sets ablaze with its flame the soul who offers me her restless longing without any physical tears. These, I tell you, are tears of fire, and this is how the Holy Spirit weeps. Since the soul cannot do it with tears, she offers her desire to weep for love of me. And if you open your mind's eye you will see that the Holy Spirit weeps in the person of every one of my servants who offers me the fragrance of holy desire and constant humble prayer. This, it seems, is what the glorious apostle Paul meant when he said that the Holy Spirit weeps before me the Father "with unspeakable groaning" for you.

(D 91)

I have told you how tears well up from the heart: The heart gathers them up from its burning desire and holds them out to the eyes. Just as green wood, when it is put into the fire, weeps tears of water in the heat because it is still green (for if it were dry it would not weep), so does the heart weep when it is made green again by the renewal of grace, after the desiccating dryness of selfishness has been drawn out of the soul. Thus are fire and tears made one in burning desire. And because desire has no end it cannot be satisfied in this life. Rather, the more it loves, the less it seems to itself to love. So love exerts a holy longing, and with that longing the eyes weep.

So your desire is an infinite thing. Were it not, could I be served by any finite thing, no virtue would have value or life. For I who am infinite God want you to serve me with what is infinite, and you have nothing infinite except your soul's love and desire.

(D 92)

The Joy of Heaven

By the same principle, those just souls who end in loving charity and are bound by love can no longer grow in virtue once time has passed. But they can forever love with that same affection with which they came to me, and by that measure will it be measured out to them (cf. Mt 7:12). They desire me forever, and forever they possess me, so their desire is not in vain. They are hungry and satisfied, satisfied yet hungry—but they are far from bored with satiety or pained in their hunger.

Forever they rejoice in love at the sight of me, sharing in that goodness which I have in myself and which I measure out to them according to the measure of love with which they have come to me. They are established in love for me and for their neighbors.[30] And they are all united in general and special love, both of which come from one and the same charity. They rejoice and exult with the angels, and they find their places among the saints according to the different virtues in which they excelled in the world.

And though they are all joined in the bond of charity, they know a special kind of sharing with those whom they loved most closely with a special love in the world, a love through which they grew in grace and virtue. They helped each other proclaim the glory and praise of my name in themselves and in their neighbors. So now in everlasting life they have not lost that love; no, they still love and share with each other even more closely and fully, adding their love to the good of all.

For I would not have you think this special good they have is only for themselves. No, it is shared by all their just companions, my beloved children, and by all the angels. For when a soul reaches eternal life, all share in her good and she in theirs. Not that anyone's vessel can get any larger or have need of filling. They are all full and can grow no larger. But they experience a new freshness in their exultation—a mirthfulness, a jubilation, a gladness—in knowing this soul. They see that by my mercy she has been lifted up from the earth in the fullness of grace, and so they are exultant in me over the good that soul has received from my goodness.

And that soul finds joy in me and in all these souls and blessed spirits, seeing and tasting in them the sweetness of my love. Their desires are a continual cry to me for the salvation of others, for they finished their lives loving their neighbors, and they did not leave that love behind but brought it with them.[31]

(D 41)

---

30. In this chapter in which Catherine describes the joy of heaven, she shows that it is a multi-faceted joy. Firstly, there is the supreme joy of seeing God face to face; next there is the general joy all experience in others' happiness; then comes the particular mutual joy of friends; and lastly when a new person enters heaven all know a fresh joy.
31. Catherine makes the special point that those in heaven do not forget about those on earth, but rather, pray continuously for them.

But after the soul has let go of the body's heaviness, her will is filled. She longed to see me and now she sees me, and in that vision is blessedness. Seeing me she knows me. Knowing me she loves me. Loving me she enjoys me, the supreme eternal Good. This enjoyment fills and satisfies her will, her longing to see me and know me. She longs for what she possesses and possesses what she longs for, and, as I have told you, her desire knows no pain, nor her satisfaction any boredom.

So you see, my servants' chief happiness is in seeing and knowing me. This vision and knowledge fills their will: They have what their will longs for and so they are satisfied. This is why I told you that, most especially, the joy of eternal life is in possessing what the will longs for. But know that its satisfaction is in seeing and knowing me. Even in this life they enjoy the pledge of eternal life, since they have a taste of the very thing that satisfies them.

(D 45)

You see, then, how the saints and all souls who have eternal life are desirous of the salvation of souls, but without pain. Their death put an end to their pain, but not to their loving charity. Indeed, they will pass through the narrow gate drunk, as it were, with the blood of the spotless Lamb, dressed in charity for their neighbors and bathed in the blood of Christ crucified, and they will find themselves in me, the sea of peace, lifted above imperfection and emptiness into perfection and filled with every good.

(D 82)

Song of Gratitude[32]

Thanks, thanks be to you, eternal Father, that you have not despised me, your handiwork, nor turned your face from me, nor made

---

32. This song occurs in the last chapter of the *Dialogue* and sums up most of the themes dealt with in the book.

light of these desires of mine. You, Light, have disregarded my darksomeness; you, Life, have not considered that I am death; nor you, Doctor, considered these grave weaknesses of mine. You, eternal Purity, have disregarded my wretched filthiness; you who are infinite have overlooked the fact that I am finite, and you, Wisdom, the fact that I am foolishness.[33] For all these and so many other endless evils and sins of mine, your wisdom, your kindness, your mercy, your infinite goodness have not despised me. No, in your light you have given me light (cf. Ps 36:10). In your wisdom I have come to know the truth; in your mercy I have found your charity and affection for my neighbors. What has compelled you? Not my virtues, but only your charity.

Let this same love compel you to enlighten the eye of my understanding with the light of faith, so that I may know your truth, which you have revealed to me. Let my memory be great enough to hold your favors, and set my will ablaze in your charity's fire. Let that fire burst the seed of my body and bring forth blood; then with that blood, given for love of your blood, and with the key of obedience, let me unlock heaven's gate.

I heartily ask the same of you for every reasoning creature, all and each of them, and for the mystic body of holy Church. I acknowledge and do not deny that you loved me before I existed, and that you love me unspeakably much, as one gone mad over your creature.

O eternal Trinity! O Godhead! That Godhead, your divine nature, gave the price of your Son's blood its value. You, eternal Trinity, are a deep sea: The more I enter you, the more I discover, and the more I discover, the more I seek you. You are insatiable, you in whose depth the soul is sated yet remains always hungry for you, thirsty for you, eternal Trinity, longing to see you with the light in your light. Just as the deer longs for the fountain of living water, so does my soul long to escape from the prison of my darksome body and see you in truth. O how long will you hide your face from my eyes? (Ps 42:2-3).

O eternal Trinity, fire and abyss of charity, dissolve this very day the cloud of my body! I am driven to desire, in the knowledge of yourself that you have given me in your truth, to leave behind the weight of this body of mine and give my life for the glory and praise

___

33. Catherine likes to use sharp contrasts to highlight the difference between Creator and creature.

of your name. For by the light of understanding within your light I have tasted and seen your depth, eternal Trinity, and the beauty of your creation. Then, when I considered myself in you, I saw that I am your image. You have gifted me with power from yourself, eternal Father, and my understanding with your wisdom—such wisdom as is proper to your only-begotten Son; and the Holy Spirit, who proceeds from you and from your Son, has given me a will, and so I am able to love.

You, eternal Trinity, are the craftsman; and I your handiwork have come to know that you are in love with the beauty of what you have made, since you made of me a new creation in the blood of your Son.

O abyss! O eternal Godhead! O deep sea! What more could you have given me than the gift of your very self?

You are a fire always burning but never consuming; you are a fire consuming in your heat all the soul's selfish love; you are a fire lifting all chill and giving light. In your light you have made me know your truth: You are that light beyond all light who gives the mind's eye supernatural light in such fullness and perfection that you bring clarity even to the light of faith. In that faith I see that my soul has life, and in that light receives you who are Light.

In the light of faith I gain wisdom in the wisdom of the Word your Son; in the light of faith I am strong, constant, persevering; in the light of faith I have hope: It does not let me faint along the way. This light teaches me the way, and without this light I would be walking in the dark. This is why I asked you, eternal Father, to enlighten me with the light of most holy faith.

Truly this light is a sea, for it nourishes the soul in you, peaceful sea, eternal Trinity. Its water is not sluggish; so the soul is not afraid because she knows the truth. It distills, revealing hidden things, so that here, where the most abundant light of your faith abounds, the soul has, as it were, a guarantee of what she believes. This water is a mirror in which you, eternal Trinity, grant me knowledge; for when I look into this mirror, holding it in the hand of love, it shows me myself, as your creation, in you, and you in me through the union you have brought about of the Godhead with our humanity.

This light shows you to me, and in this light I know you, highest and infinite Good: Good above every good, joyous Good, Good beyond measure and understanding! Beauty above all beauty; Wisdom above all wisdom—indeed you are wisdom itself! You who are the angels' food are given to humans with burning love. You, garment who cover all nakedness, pasture the starving within your sweetness, for you are sweet without trace of bitterness.

O eternal Trinity, when I received with the light of most holy faith your light that you gave me, I came to know therein the way of great perfection, made smooth for me by so many wonderful explanations. Thus I may serve you in the light, not in the dark; and I may be a mirror of a good and holy life; and I may rouse myself from my wretched life in which, always through my own fault, I have served you in darkness. I did not know your truth, and so I did not love it. Why did I not know you? Because I did not see you with the glorious light of most holy faith, since the cloud of selfish love darkened the eye of my understanding. Then with your light, eternal Trinity, you dispelled the darkness.

But who could reach to your height to thank you for so immeasurable a gift, for such generous favors, for the teaching of truth that you have given me? A special grace, this, beyond the common grace you give to other creatures. You willed to bend down to my need and that of others who might see themselves mirrored here.

You responded, Lord; you yourself have given and you yourself answered and satisfied me by flooding me with a gracious light, so that with that light I may return thanks to you. Clothe, clothe me with yourself, eternal Truth, so that I may run the course of this mortal life in true obedience and in the light of most holy faith. With that light I sense my soul once again becoming drunk! Thanks be to God! Amen.

(D 167)

Chronology

1347 25 March: Catherine, with her twin sister Giovanna, is born in Siena to the cloth-dyer Jacopo Benincasa and his wife Lapa di Puccio Piagenti. Giovanna dies shortly afterward.

1348 Outbreak of the Black Death in Siena.

1353 Returning from her brother Stefano's house, Catherine has a vision of Christ over the church of San Domenico. Although she is very young, this vision affects her greatly and influences her decision to give her life to God and to work for the renewal of the Church.

1354 Catherine makes a vow of virginity.

1362 Her favorite sister, Bonaventura, dies. This event leads Catherine to a conversion experience in which she commits her life to God in a more complete way. The Dominican friar Tommaso della Fonte becomes her confessor and guide.

1363 (or 1364) Catherine joins the Mantellate, a group of Dominican laywomen in Siena, and begins a three-year period of living in almost complete seclusion at home. During this period she learns to read.

1367 During prayer Catherine has the experience of mystical espousal in faith to Christ. Shortly afterward she leaves her seclusion and begins a life of active service of others, particularly the sick and the poor.

1368 Catherine's father dies. A "family" of followers begins to form around her.

1370 Famine hits Siena. In July and August Catherine enjoys a series of intense mystical experiences, which culminate in her "mystical death." This last gives her a new enthusiasm to bring the message of Christ to others.

1372 Her political activity begins. This mostly takes the form of peace-making efforts on behalf of various Italian states.

1374 Catherine makes her first visit to Florence where at a General Chapter of the Dominican Order Raymond of Capua is assigned to her as confessor and guide. In May a fresh outbreak of the Black Death hits Siena. Catherine devotes herself to caring for the sick and dying.

1375 For most of this year she is in Pisa preaching a crusade and working for reconciliation between city-states and the papacy. In April she receives the stigmata in the church of Santa Cristina in Pisa. In the summer she returns briefly to Siena to visit and help the condemned prisoner, Niccolò di Toldo.

1376 Florence is placed under papal interdict. At the request of the Florentines Catherine travels with some companions to Avignon to mediate with Pope Gregory XI on their behalf. She is also concerned with the return of the pope to Rome and with Church reform. On 13 September Gregory XI leaves Avignon for Rome. Catherine and her followers depart for Siena by a different route.

1377 The pope reaches Rome in January. Catherine founds a monastery for nuns at Belcaro near Siena. She spends most of April there. In the early summer she goes with several of her disciples to Val d'Orcia on an evangelizing mission which lasts until Advent. While she is away her friend Raymond leaves Siena having been appointed prior of the Dominican convent attached to the church of the Minerva in Rome. Catherine learns to write and begins work on her *Dialogue* around October. By December she is back in Siena.

1378 (or December 1377) Catherine is sent to Florence by the pope to mediate peace. She continues working on her *Dialogue*. Gregory XI dies on 27 March and his successor, Urban VI, is elected on 8 April. Very soon afterward schism begins to threaten the Church. In June, still in Florence, Catherine is almost assassinated when riots break out in the city. At the end of July peace is declared between Florence and the papacy and she returns to Siena. There she devotes herself to her *Dialogue* completing it in October. The great schism begins in the Church on 20 September when the dissatisfied cardinals elect the antipope, Clement VII. Catherine is firm and active in her support of Urban VI, who in November summons her to Rome to work for his cause. She brings a number of her companions with her, and together they begin living as a community in a house near the Minerva. She has hardly arrived there, however, when her friend and guide, Raymond, is sent on a mission to France by the pope. She never sees him again.

1379 In Rome Catherine devotes all her energy to the cause of the unity of the Church. She spends hours in prayer for this intention, and she sends letters and messengers to many parts of the Christian world in support of the true pope. She falls into ill-health. Most of her recorded prayers belong to this period.

1380 At the beginning of this year her health deteriorates badly. She can no longer eat or drink, but she still "drags herself" each day to St. Peter's, a mile away, to spend the time in prayer for the Church. She undergoes terrifying moral and physical trials. She still manages to dictate letters on behalf of Church unity. On 26 February she loses the use of her legs and is confined to the house. She offers her life for the Church. She dies after much suffering in the presence of many of her "family" on 29 April.

Selected Bibliography

The Works of Catherine of Siena

The Dialogue

Cavallini, Giuliana, ed. *Il dialogo della divina provvidenza*. Rome: Edizioni Cateriniane, 1968.

Noffke, Suzanne, trans. *Catherine of Siena: The Dialogue*. New York: Paulist Press, 1980.

The Letters

Dupré Theseider, Eugenio, ed. *Epistolario di S. Caterina da Siena*. Rome: Istituto Storico Italiano, 1940.

Foster, Kenelm and Ronayne, Mary John, eds. and transl. *I Catherine*. London: Collins, 1980.

Gigli, Girolamo, ed. *Le opere di S. Caterina da Siena*. 4 vols. Siena and Lucca, 1707-21.

Misciattelli, Piero, ed. *Le lettere di S. Caterina da Siena*. Annotated by Niccolò Tommaseo. 6 vols. Siena: Giuntini and Bentivoglio, 1913-22.

Noffke, Suzanne, trans. *The Letters of St. Catherine of Siena*. 2 vols. Tempe: Arizona Center for Medieval and Renaissance Studies, 2000-2001 (more volumes to follow).

Scudder, Vida, ed. and transl. *St. Catherine of Siena as Seen in Her Letters*. New York: E. P. Dutton, 1927.

The Prayers

Cavallini, Giuliana, ed. *Le orazioni di S. Caterina da Siena*. Rome: Edizioni Cateriniane, 1978.

Noffke, Suzanne, trans. *The Prayers of Catherine of Siena*. New York: Paulist Press, 1983.

Biographical Sources

Drane, Augusta. *The History of St. Catherine of Siena and Her Companions*. 2 vols. London: Burns, Oates and Washbourne, 1914.

Fawtier, Robert. *Sainte Catherine de Sienne, Essai de critique des sources: I. Sources hagiographiques*. Paris: Boccard, 1921.

Gardner, E. G. *Saint Catherine of Siena*. London: J. M. Dent, 1907.

Jorgensen, Johannes. *Saint Catherine of Siena*. Translated by I. Lund. London: Longmans, Green and Co., 1938.

Laurent, M.-H., ed. *Fontes vitae S. Catharinae Senensis historici IX, Il Processo Castellano*. Milan: Bocca, 1942.

Raimondo da Capua. *Legenda Maior.* Translated by G. Tinagli. Siena: Cantagalli, 1934. English translations by G. Lamb. *The Life of St. Catherine of Siena.* London: Harvill Press, 1960; and C. Kearns. *The Life of Catherine of Siena by Raymond of Capua.* Wilmington: Michael Glazier, 1980.

Thomas Antonii de Senis "Caffarini."*Libellus de supplemento.* Edited by G. Cavallini and I. Foraloso. Rome: Edizioni Cateriniane, 1974.

_____. *Legenda Minor.* Edited by E. Francischini. Milan: Bocca, 1942.

Theological Studies

Ashley, Benedict. "Guide to St. Catherine's Dialogue." *Cross and Crown* 29 (1977): 237-49.

Cavallini, Giuliana. "Dottrina dell'amore in S. Caterina da Siena: concordanze col pensiero di S. Tommaso d'Aquino." *Divus Thomas* LXXV (1972): 369-88.

_____. "Fonti neotestamentarie degli scritti cateriniani." *Atti del Congresso Internazionale di Studi Cateriniani.* Rome: Curia Generalizia O.P., 1981, 44-59.

D'Urso, Giacinto, *Il genio di Santa Caterina: Studi sulla sua dottrina e personalità.* Rome: Edizioni Cateriniane, 1971.

Foster, Kenelm. "The Spirit of St. Catherine of Siena." *Life of the Spirit* 15 (1961): 433-46.

_____. "St. Catherine's Teaching on Christ." *Life of the Spirit* 16 (1962): 310-23.

Garrigou-Lagrange, R. "La foi selon sainte Catherine de Sienne." *La Vie Spirituelle* 44 (1935): 236-49.

_____. "La charité selon sainte Catherine de Sienne." *La Vie Spirituelle* 47 (1936): 29-44.

_____. "L'espérance selon sainte Catherine de Sienne." *La Vie Spirituelle* 49 (1936): 225-37.

Grion, Alvaro. *La dottrina di Santa Caterina da Siena.* Brescia: Morcelliana, 1962.

John Paul II. *Amantissima Providentia.* "Apostolic Letter on the 6th Centenary of the Death of St. Catherine of Siena." *L'Osservatore Romano* II (1980).

Kearns, Conleth. "The Wisdom of St. Catherine." *Angelicum* 57 (1980): 324-43.

Noffke, Suzanne. "Catherine of Siena, Justly Doctor of the Church." *Theology Today* 60 (2003):49-62.

O'Driscoll, Mary. "Mercy for the World: St. Catherine's View of Intercessory Prayer." *Spirituality Today* 32, 1 (1980): 36-45.

_____. "Catherine the Theologian." *Spirituality Today* 40, 1 (1988): 4-17.

_____. "The Lived Theology of Catherine of Siena." *Doctrine and Life* 54,4 (April 2004):13-25.